WU STYLE TAI CHI CHUAN
ANCIENT CHINESE WAY TO HEALTH

DR. WEN ZEE

徐文醫師近作

用科学态度和方法

研究太极拳

九二叟

馬岳梁題

MASTER MA'S CALLIGRAPHY
To Dr. Wen Zee,
Using scientific method for the research work of Tai chi chuan.
　　　　—Ma Yueh-liang, at the age of 92

WU STYLE TAI CHI CHUAN
ANCIENT CHINESE WAY TO HEALTH

DR. WEN ZEE

With forewords by
The Late Grandmaster Ma Yueh-liang
and
Andrew Weil, M.D.

NORTH ATLANTIC BOOKS
Berkeley, California

Published by
North Atlantic Books
P.O. Box 12327
Berkeley, California 94712

Cover and book design by Jennifer Dunn
Printed in the United States of America

Wu Style Tai Chi Chuan: Ancient Chinese Way to Health is sponsored by the Society for the Study of Native Arts and Sciences, a nonprofit educational corporation whose goals are to develop an educational and crosscultural perspective linking various scientific, social, and artistic fields; to nurture a holistic view of arts, sciences, humanities, and healing; and to publish and distribute literature on the relationship of mind, body, and nature.

North Atlantic Books are available through most bookstores. To contact North Atlantic directly, call 800-337-2665 or visit our website at www.northatlanticbooks.com.

Substantial discounts on bulk quantities of North Atlantic books are available to corporations, professional associations, and other organizations. For details and discount information, contact the special sales department at North Atlantic Books.

Library of Congress Cataloging-in-Publication Data

Zee, Wen.
    Wu style tai chi chuan : ancient Chinese way to health / by Wen Zee.
        p. cm.
    ISBN 1-55642-389-1 (pbk.)

GV504 .Z44 2002
613.7/148 21

1   2   3   4   5   6   /   06   05   04   03   02

Table of Contents

Foreword

Think what the final purpose is . . .
Longevity with eternal spring.
—*The Chant of the Thirteen Kinetic Movements*

This verse was written in the tai chi Classics and states the principal purpose of practicing tai chi chuan, which is to prolong life and maintain well-being, not solely to obtain martial skill. "Eternal spring" refers to a person's ability to live with great vigor and joy well into his eighties and nineties.

Longevity is the goal everyone seeks, but most important is the continued integration of health with old age. What is the use of living longer if one suffers from chronic diseases or general debilitation and must be cared for like a small child?

"How delightful to see a man in his eighties able to ward off crowds!" states Wang Zhong-yueh, author of *The Treatise of Tai Chi Chuan*, describing how a tai chi master can maintain good health, vigor, and quick reflexes. This helps one enjoy life more completely in all respects.

In modern society, people live in a tense and busy physical and mental state. Completing a full set of tai chi chuan helps reduce stress and promote one's spirit, and allows recovery from fatigue and the worries of everyday life. Innumerable tai chi practitioners have experienced all the health benefits described in this book. In recent years, articles in prestigious journals from around the Western world have begun to scientifically document many of the well-known health benefits of tai chi chuan.

Dr. Wen Zee has studied tai chi chuan with me since he was a teenage student in high school, interrupted only by war and other difficult times. Starting in the 1950s, he worked in government hospitals in Shanghai as a clinical doctor for almost thirty years. Although he was

Master Ma and Dr. Zee at Ma's home

busy with his medical career, he continued his tai chi practice and his research into the medical benefits of tai chi chuan, with especially encouraging results for his patients with heart disease and hypertension.

The use of scientific methods to determine the mechanisms of the healing effects of tai chi chuan is vital and should be based upon rigorous physiological testing. For many years, exercise has been seen as a mechanistic concept in the West, and people have generally exercised using machines and by doing repeated mechanical work. Tai chi is different. It is a mind-body exercise for the twenty-first century. Since the restoration of the Chian Chuan Tai Chi Chuan Association of Shanghai in 1980, Dr. Zee has been studying and working with me even more closely. We are the co-authors of the book *Push Hands,* which was published in both Chinese and English in Hong Kong. He also edited and translated into English my book *Wu-Style Taichichuan: Forms, Concepts and Application of the Original Style,* which is well-known in the tai chi community of the United States, Germany, Australia, and areas in Southeast Asia.

Tai chi uses the mind, not force. The mind directs the *qi* (pronounced chee), and the qi directs the body. In the tai chi Classics, it says, "Our mind is the master, and the muscles and bones are the servants."

Tai chi is whole-body movement. The internal qi and the external forms must coordinate in harmony and move as one entity. It is critical that the forms be performed precisely. If the external forms are done incorrectly, the internal qi cannot link joint by joint throughout the body.

The publication of this book not only provides examples of the modern and scientific use of tai chi chuan, but also helps the reader to learn the authentic Wu-style tai chi chuan, which was passed down from the late grandmaster Wu Chian Chuan.

      —Grandmaster Ma Yueh-liang
       (At the age of 96)

Foreword

Most Americans familiar with tai chi know it only as "Chinese shadow-boxing," a soft martial art that thousands of people practice every morning in city parks in China. Actually, tai chi is an ancient mind-body practice which maintains and enhances health and longevity by directing life energy (known as qi) around the body. Like many Eastern esoteric practices, it has been passed on as a tradition from master to student and is not easily learned from books, even when these have been available in English.

One of the great modern teachers of tai chi was grandmaster Ma Yueh-liang, who died in 1998 at the age of 98. Late in his life and still in vigorous health, he became well-known in the West because of his appearance in a widely seen public television program and subsequent book, *Healing and the Mind,* produced by Bill Moyers. The author of the present book, Dr. Wen Zee, was a lifelong student of Master Ma. Dr. Zee began studying with Ma at the age of 17. Eventually, he co-authored two books with him and became the trustee of the Wu-Style Tai Chi Association of Shanghai that Ma directed. Dr. Zee has been the principal teacher of authentic Wu-style tai chi in America.

I have known Dr. Zee since he began training people of all ages in my hometown of Tucson, Arizona, ten years ago. Recently, I asked him to teach tai chi to the physicians enrolled in the Program in Integrative Medicine I direct at the University of Arizona College of Medicine. As a physician trained in Western medicine, I am interested not so much in qi energy as I am in the health benefits of this practice in terms that I understand. I think those benefits are many.

Tai chi improves flexibility and balance, qualities of young bodies we want to protect and maintain as we age. The aged who practice tai chi are less likely to fall, and if they do fall are less likely to sustain serious injuries. Since falls are a major cause of disability and death in the aged, anything that reduces their frequency and consequences is valuable.

Tai chi is also an effective relaxation technique. Its slow, graceful movements and emphasis on breath and mind control produce a relaxation response, which can be marked by decreased blood pressure and heart rate, as well as improved circulation and digestion. Not only is it useful for neutralizing the harmful effects of stress, it can treat a range of chronic illnesses rooted in unbalanced functioning of the autonomic nervous system.

It may be less obvious that tai chi contributes to the long-term health of bones as well as muscles. As Dr. Zee points out, when the muscles are relaxed, the whole body weight lies on the bones, which become stronger as a result. Thus, tai chi can help prevent osteoporosis, which is another leading cause of disability in the elderly.

These benefits are documented in medical research conducted in the West through collaborations between physicians and teachers of authentic tai chi styles such as Dr. Zee.

One of the main thrusts of integrative medicine is to identify and incorporate into mainstream medicine natural techniques that can enhance the body's own mechanisms of healing. Tai chi is such a technique, and I am grateful to Dr. Wen Zee for spreading knowledge of it here. His book presents a wealth of detail about the health benefits of tai chi as well as useful information about the philosophical theory underlying it and the basics of practice. I am happy to introduce it to American readers.

—Andrew Weil, M.D.
Tucson, Arizona
December 2000

CHAPTER 1

The Philosophy of Tai Chi

That which circulates is the qi.
That which dominates is the principle.
That which contrasts is the numerical.

MORE THAN TWO THOUSAND YEARS AGO in ancient China, when Confucius was watching the water in the upper reach of a river, he exclaimed, "Is not all that passed like this? Day and night without end!" Likewise, the ancient Greek philosopher Heraclitus (540–480 B.C.) said, "You cannot step in the same water of the river twice."

In the 1950s when I was a resident doctor working in the prestigious Shanghai Number Six People's Hospital, I read Dr. Paul White's book *Heart Disease.* Inside the cover of the book, written by the noted cardiologist who cared for Dwight Eisenhower after the president suffered a heart attack, was a quotation: "Man's life is a chain of chances."

These simple words made a deep and lasting impression on me. A medical resident's life is much the same the world over: long hours, little sleep, and heart-rending medical triumphs and tragedies. It is an intense and meaningful period in a young person's life, ripe for philosophical thoughts, and White's words came to me at a time when I was receptive to them. This one brief sentence contains the idea that a man's life, as well as all things in the universe, is constantly moving and changing and involved in a supremely dynamic flux. At that time in my naiveté, I believed that a person's success depended largely on chance. Now I know better.

I later came to understand that everything in the universe is indeed in a state of everlasting movement and change. Changes are innumerable, so are chances. There are certain universally applicable rules that explain all the changes of Nature, not only in the physical world, but in human society as well. These rules are the theory of *yin-yang*.

The body is an integrated whole, yet its parts are also constantly moving and changing according to the theory of yin-yang. Since the human body is the creation of Nature, the human body and the universe can be considered one entity. Thus, the ancient Chinese believed that following the way of Nature, based on the theory of yin-yang, was the way to maintain health and longevity.

The philosophy of *I-Ching* is the root of all Chinese culture. Our morals, ethics, and ancient arts and sciences—including astronomy, war craft, medicine, architecture, music, painting, and *feng shui*—have been stamped with its imprint. Among these, too, is the ancient Chinese martial art of tai chi, which could only have been developed in China, because its philosophy is a branch of the same ancient root as the indigenous philosophy enshrined in the *I-Ching*.

In *The Ten Introductory Chapters of I-Ching*, said to have been written by Confucius, it is said:

> When Fuxi had come to rule all under heaven, looking up, he contemplated brilliant forms in the sky, and looking down he surveyed patterns shown on the earth. He contemplated the ornamental appearances of the birds and beasts and different suitabilities of the soil. Near at hand, in his own body, he found changes for consideration, and at a distance he examined things in general. Finally he devised the eight trigrams to show fully the attributes of all the mysteries and to classify the qualities of myriad things.

Fuxi was a legendary emperor and saint who lived in ancient China about five thousand years ago, before the invention of the Chinese characters. Some historians believe that the trigrams are the embryonic or primitive forms of the Chinese characters.

The eight trigrams are groups of figures or diagrams formed by three horizontal lines. The lines are either solid (—) or broken, (– –). The solid line represents yang and the odd numbers; the broken line represents yin and the even numbers. The yin and yang lines are termed the *yoa*. Each diagram is formed by three yoa, so there are eight possible trigrams. If you combine any two trigrams, you can construct a new diagram composed of six yoa. There are 64 doubled or overlapping trigrams altogether. All the changes in the universe can be explained by the changing of yin and yang. Therefore, the changing of yin and yang yoa as you go from one of the 64 overlapping trigrams to another can be used not only to explain the present and the past, but also to predict the future.

Thus, the 64 overlapping trigrams are often used as symbols for divination. In reality, the philosophy of *I-Ching* is the mainstream of Chinese culture, the crystallizing of the wits of the ancient Chinese people.

Two thousand years after Fuxi's time, Emperor Wen of the Zhou dynasty (1100 B.C.) composed the explanations of the eight trigrams. He interpreted the meanings and attributes of every yin and yang yoa in each diagram.

Five hundred years after Emperor Wen's time, Confucius wrote *The Ten Introductory Chapters,* known as *The Ten Wings of I-Ching.* The three main components of *I-Ching* are: the eight trigrams of Fuxi, the explanations of the diagrams by Emperor Wen, and *The Ten Wings* of Confucius. An ancient verse says, "How profound the *I-Ching* is! It was completed in three ancient stages and worked out by three sages."

The term *tai chi* is first encountered in *The Ten Wings of I-Ching* where Confucius wrote, "What the *I-Ching* deals with is tai chi, which gives birth to two elementary forms. The two forms give birth to four phases and, again, the eight trigrams." The word *tai* literally means "the greatest," and *chi* "the ultimate." The term *tai chi* can be explained as the grand terminus no one can go beyond. Tai chi is by no means a religious term. It tells you the ultimate reality, how all things in the universe change and happen.

The term *wu chi* was first written in the *Tao Te Ching* by Lao-tzu. The word *wu* verbally means "no," so *wu chi* means "no terminus." It is wrong to say that tai chi is created from wu chi. If wu chi created tai chi, then what created wu chi? Actually, the two words have the same meaning.

In Taoism, the term *tai yi* is a synonym for tai chi. The word *yi* in Chinese means "one." *Tai yi* means "the greatest one," or the Grand Wholeness. As written by Lao-tzu in *Tao Te Ching,* one creates two—the yin and yang—two create three, and the three create all things in the universe.

Nei Ching, the classic of Chinese traditional medicine, also called *The Yellow Emperor's Classic of Internal Medicine* (427–421 B.C.), states, "Yin-yang is the Tao of heaven and earth, the outline and discipline of all things, the origin of birth and death and the source of all mysteries."

The symbol of tai chi (Figure 1) is the dynamic model of the theory of yin-yang. First, observe that the symbol is a circle, which denotes that all things in the universe are one entity. The curve in the middle implies that all things in the universe are constantly moving and changing. Also, if you draw a line through the center from any part of the circle, the amount of yin and yang in each half of the circle is always quantitatively equal. This shows that yin and yang are always in balance. If they are not in balance, it will undermine the constant movement of the universe.

FIGURE 1
The Symbol of Tai Chi

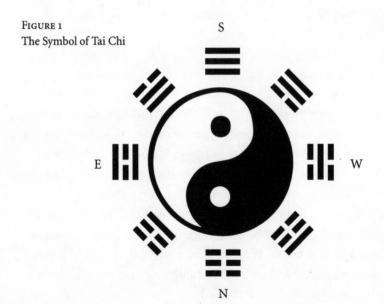

When yang increases, yin decreases; when yin increases, yang decreases. They wax and wane in unison. The yang having reached its climax retreats in favor of yin, and the yin having reached its climax retreats in favor of yang. This means that when things reach their extremity, they turn to their opposite.

This cyclical movement produces the four phases called the junior yang and the senior yang, and the junior yin and the senior yin. These phases may represent the four seasons of spring, summer, autumn, and winter. Time is created by movement; time and space can be considered as one entity. Time has no beginning and no end, and space is neither big nor small, but both can only be expressed relatively in numerical terms.

The black dot in the white and the white dot in the black means that the yang contains yin and the yin contains yang.

Yang represents the nature of heaven, the sun, masculinity, hardness, movement, and subjectivity. It is the ceaseless initiator. Yin represents the nature of the earth, the moon, femininity, softness, and objectivity. Yin is silent and still, but it ceaselessly interacts with the movement of yang through induction. It is receptive, adaptive, and creative. Since the yang is constantly moving, absolute stillness of yin does not exist.

The exercise form tai chi is commonly called tai chi chuan in China. The word *chuan* means "fist," and it emphasizes the martial aspect of tai chi, which is one of the soft, internal martial arts (as opposed to the hard, external Chinese martial arts, or *kung-fu*). The final purpose of tai chi, as expressed in the Classics, is longevity and eternal spring. Eternal spring means that persistent practice will lead to a healthier and longer life. You will remain energetic, flexible, have good balance, and maintain quick reflexes even as you get older.

CHAPTER 2

The Origin of Tai Chi Chuan

Returning to the historical reality,
based on extensive research by the author.

ARTISTIC TECHNIQUES are always created within certain cultural and historical contexts, and through common societal usage such techniques develop and mature. The five thousand-year history and splendid culture of China have created the diverse, substantial, and highly practical traditional martial arts. Influences of ancient ethics and philosophy are also characteristic of the Chinese martial arts.

Chinese martial arts were likely classified as early as the 17th century as being either of the internal school or the external school. The well-known scholar, Wang Li-zhou (A.D. 1610–1695), who lived at the end of the Ming dynasty and the beginning of the Qing dynasty, stated in one of his essays, "There is now the so-called internal martial arts, which is to overcome the offensive with stillness. The enemy often was thrown to the ground at the first touch of the hands. This is different from Shao-ling, the hard external school." With this statement, the terms "internal" and "external" martial arts are first found in written literature.

The soft school of Chinese martial arts is derived from the hard style. Martial artists, as they got older, tended to change from hard to soft in different degrees. This change resulted from using internal force rather than external strength, from using craft or technique rather than raw power, and by transforming from an antagonistic state to a neutralizing or diverting state when confronting an enemy. This could be the sublimation of long-term practice of martial arts, the decreased energy brought on by the aging process, or a combination of the two. Tai chi chuan belongs to the internal school, and it is evident that it was transformed from traditional Chinese martial arts. There are strong similarities between the palm patterns, postures, foot stances, and some of the basic rules of traditional hard martial arts and tai chi. In *The Classic of Martial Arts*, written by General Qi Ji-guan (1528–1587), who was well-known for fighting the Japanese invaders during the Ming dynasty, some postures are featured which, when compared to the postures in the book of Xu Yi-seng (1879–1945), *Explanation of Postures of Tai Chi Chuan*, show great similarity or even duplication in shape, name, and stance. This information proves that tai chi chuan is derived from traditional Chinese martial arts.

FIGURE 1
The similarity between General Qi Ji-guan and Xu Yi-seng featured postures.

1   2   3   4   5

The pictures in the book, *The Classic of Martial Arts,* by General Qi Ji-guan.

1. Seven Star Position
2. Double Changing Legs
3. Twist Single Whip
4. Pointing to the Crotch Punch
5. Golden Cockerel Standing on One Leg

1   2   3   4   5

The pictures in the book, *Explanations of The Postures Of Tai Chi Chuan,* By Xu Yi-seng.

1. Seven Star Method
2. Double Kicking
3. Single Whip
4. Pointing to the Crotch Punch
5. Golden Cockerel Standing on One Leg

Xu Yi-seng was a Yang stylist who established the Athletic Research Institute in Beijing during the early stage of the Republic of China.

The Classic of Martial Arts by General Qi Ji-guan also features a collection of different and well-known martial arts during the period from the Sung to the Ming dynasty. There is not a single word about tai chi in this book, which proves that before the 16th century, tai chi chuan did not exist. Tai chi chuan could only have developed after the period of General Qi Ji-guan.

This information is reinforced by the book *Methods of Internal Martial Arts,* by Wang Bai-chia, son of Wang Li-zhou, which does not mention tai chi chuan. It is reasonable to state, therefore, that in the end of the Ming dynasty and the beginning of the Qing dynasty, although there was an internal school of martial arts, systematic tai chi chuan did not exist.

In the late 17th and 18th centuries, during the so-called "prosperous time" under the reign of the Emperor Kang Xy (1662–1722) and especially under the reign of Emperor Qian-loong (1736–1795) of the Qing dynasty, all aspects of the arts flourished. The long-term stability of political conditions under this regime resulted in an economic and cultural boom, and the frequent contact of people traveling from different regions increased the level of cultural exchange. Such locales as Lao Yang, Kai Fen, Yi Sui, and Wen County, known as Central China at this time, were famed as places where martial arts flourished. These martial artists influenced and transformed the different martial art forms and created many new categories of internal and external schools. At this time, the internal martial artists, under the guidance of the yin-yang theory in the *Book of Changes* and Taoist experience regarding longevity and healing, gave birth to the system of integrated tai chi chuan. This unique exercise system, which can be used for self-defense and as a way to maintain health, continues to be enriched and integrated through long-term social usage and practice. Tai chi chuan was not created by an immortal, as some legends have it. Nor did it result from an individual's observation of a crane and snake locked in mortal combat. The variety and profoundness of the methods, postures, and philosophy could not have been created by any one person or during any one lifetime. Indeed, tai chi chuan is the creation of ancient Chinese culture and history, the sublimation of traditional Chinese martial arts, and the crystallization of the wit of the Chinese people.

China was ruled by the Mongolians during the Yuan dynasty (1271–1368), and then by the Manchurians during the Qing dynasty (1646–1911), a period from the mid-17th century to the early 20th century. Because each of these ruling classes was but a small portion of the entire population and feared uprising among the people, they controlled all weapons. The instruction and circulation of information regarding martial arts were also strictly forbidden to the common people. This gap in the free exchange of information regarding martial arts makes it especially difficult to research texts on the subject.

However, thanks to the few historical documents published in the Ming dynasty and beyond, some logical conclusions can be reached regarding the still-controversial people who were critical to the development of tai chi chuan. It is necessary to discuss these individuals to present a factual report on the role each played in the history of this art.

CHANG SAN-FENG: IS HE THE FOUNDER OF TAI CHI CHUAN?

Chang San-feng was born in 1247, lived during the Yuan and Ming dynasties, and probably lived to reach 110 years of age. When he was young, he was a Confucian scholar. After his parents' death, he became a Taoist monk, leaving his family and roaming over much of China during his life. At 70 years of age, he settled in the Wu Dan Mountains in central China for much of the rest of his life. He represents the unity of the three religions: Buddhism, Taoism, and Confucianism, which created the Wu Dan school of Taoism. Chang San-feng was known as both a great alchemist, making pills from metals to attain immortality, and a great poet, with poems selected and published in the Great Encyclopedia of the Ming dynasty of Emperor Yung Lao.

During the past two hundred years, it has been common knowledge that the Chinese martial arts are divided into two main groups— the Wu Dan school and the Shao-ling school. The former, known as the soft internal school, originated with the Taoist monks of the Wu Dan

FIGURE 2
Picture of the statue of
Chang San-feng in Shaanxi
Province in Northwest
China, where he once lived.

Mountain region. The latter, known as the hard external school, originated with the Buddhist monks of the Shao-ling Temple in Henan Province. These two areas have been known for so long as Meccas of the martial arts, there is virtually no dispute over the regional importance of each site. Chang San-feng was critical to the development of the Wu Dan school of Taoism and the Wu Dan school of martial arts.

In both the Yang and the Wu style of tai chi chuan, when a master selects an indoor disciple, a solemn ceremony takes place. An indoor disciple is one who has a common martial arts lineage with the master and completely shares the discipline. The induction ceremony begins with homage to a tablet on which is written the name of father

Chang San-feng. Placed at the center of the room, this tablet is flanked by a pair of large, brightly burning red candles. The new disciple has to kowtow, or bow deeply, first to the tablet and then to the *sifu*. A sifu is more than a teacher; his relationship with his disciple is closer in nature to that between a respected master and an apprentice.

April 9 of the Chinese lunar calendar is the birth date of Chang San-feng, and celebrations are still held on this date by several of the tai chi organizations in different places in China.

Chang San-feng is not acknowledged by some authors as the founder of tai chi chuan because he was not a famous martial artist. But none can deny that the main discipline of tai chi chuan is influenced by Taoist theory, especially the theoretical base of the maintenance of health and longevity. The famous Taoist doctrine which says "Sublimate the generative essence into qi, sublimate the qi into spirit, and sublimate the spirit into great emptiness" is also applied to tai chi chuan. Realization of this philosophy is the goal and highest realm sought by many tai chi chuan masters.

In ancient China, large temples belonging to either the Taoist or the Buddhist monks were often built deep in the scenic mountains. The monks were trained in the martial arts to protect and defend temple property. As Chang San-feng's Taoism was the predominant school during the Yuan, Ming, and Qing dynasties when tai chi chuan was being developed, the issue of his being a famous martial artist is irrelevant. In China, as in much of the world, people name a specific person as the founder of a great art, such as Sheng-nong, founder of Chinese herbal medicine; Tsai-lung, the inventor of paper; and Lu-pan, the founder of carpentry. So why not commemorate Chang San-feng as the founder of tai chi chuan?

SANYOU WANG ZHONG-YUEH, AUTHOR OF THE TREATISE OF TAI CHI CHUAN

The Treatise of Tai Chi Chuan, written by *Sanyou* Wang Zhong-yueh, is the most authoritative classic of tai chi chuan, for it contains both systematic and theoretical principles. It is treated as a bible by tai chi practitioners. This article shows the author to be not only a great tai chi master, but also a great literary talent. His work is often cited as a determining factor for qualifying a good vs. bad teacher. Although the movement and methods may differ considerably from teacher to teacher in different styles, the basic theories and principles espoused in this treatise must serve as a basis for instruction.

Sanyou Wang Zhong-yueh was critical in the development of tai chi chuan because he integrated the theoretical base of this art. Without the theoretical guidance of this classic, tai chi chuan would not have spread throughout the world. The integration of the theoretical, philosophical, and physical realms provided a path sought by vast numbers of learners.

The period in which Wang Zhong-yueh lived and wrote became an issue of controversy, for no printed matter regarding martial arts was allowed to be circulated at that time. However, the era can be deduced thanks to the original signing of the author's name. It is a Chinese custom when signing a name to list the locale of one's native land before one's given name. Sanyou is the name of a region, now known as Shanxi Province. The term *san* literally means "mountain," and *you* means "right." Therefore, *Sanyou* means "to the right of the mountain Taihang." The term *Sanzhou* means "to the left of the mountain Taihang," now known as the Sangtung province. The names Sanyou and Sanzhou were popularly used only in the Qing dynasty and in the early stages of the formation of the Republic of China. This provides strong evidence that Wang Zhong-yueh lived during the Qing dynasty and most likely during the reign of the Emperor Qian-loong.

To further validate this claim, a valuable ancient handwritten book about tai chi chuan and the spear form was discovered in a second-hand bookstore by the noted tai chi historian Tong-hau in the early 1930s. In the book, it states that there was a Sanyou master Wang, who was proficient in ancient Chinese literature and skilled in the martial arts. He lived in Laoyang in the 60th reigning year of Emperor Qian-loong of the Qing dynasty, in the year 1791. In 1795, he taught martial arts in Kai-fen during the later stages of Emperor Qian-loong's reign. This Sanyou master Wang could only be Wang Zhong-yueh.

The Treatise of Tai Chi Chuan, written by *Sanyou* Wang Zhong-yueh, was found by Hu Yi-xiang (1812–1880) in a salt shop in Wuyang

County, about one hundred miles from Hu's home in Yungnian County in Hebei Province. The time between the death of Wang Zhong-yueh and the finding of this classic is probably around fifty years. Hu Yi-xiang was a high official from a wealthy family, skilled in the martial arts. Hu was a friend of Yang Lu-chan, the grandmaster of the Yang style, who lived in the South Gate of Yungnian. Hu not only discovered the classic work by Wang Zhong-yueh, he also penned important works of his own, which added to the scarce classical literature of tai chi chuan. His tai chi chuan was later called the Hu style, which became one of the five main tai chi styles along with Yang, Wu, Chen, and Sung. According to a book published by Xu Zheng (1898–1967), another famous martial arts historian, there were no references to tai chi chuan prior to Wang Zhong-yueh's treatise.

JIANG-FA, THE MAN WHO IMPARTED TAI CHI CHUAN TO THE CHEN FAMILY

Because of a lack of valid historical records or references, Jiang-fa is also a man of great controversy. It is important to discuss Jiang-fa for two reasons. First, he is a key historical figure. Second, his recorded activities may clarify the controversy surrounding the development and propagation of tai chi chuan from the Qing dynasty to modern times—a period of approximately two hundred years. It is recognized that he was a disciple of Wang Zhong-yueh. In the early 1900s, stories about Jiang-fa were popular among the elders in Beijing.

Tong-hau, a lawyer of Shanghai, went to Chenchiakou in the 1930s to explore the place and person who created tai chi chuan. Chenchi-akou is a village of Wen County in Hebei Province that has been famous in martial arts and tai chi for several generations. When he returned to Shanghai, Tong-hau published literature stating that the Taoist monk Chang San-feng, not being a famous martial artist, could not have been the founder of tai chi chuan. Therefore, the Chen family's ancestor, Chen Wang-din, was given this honor.

A retired military official, Chen Wang-din lived in the village of Chenchiakou and taught martial arts after the end of the Ming dynasty and during the beginning of the Qing dynasty. The martial art taught by the Chen family at this time is called *pao-sui* or "cannon fist." The name tai chi chuan was never used in any of Chen Wang-din's work or poems. Before the publishing of Tong-hau's work, even the Chen family never claimed Chen Wang-din was the founder of tai chi chuan.

The term "Chen-style tai chi chuan" was openly claimed only after tai chi chuan became popular in Beijing and other parts of China. Now the Chen family states that Chenchiakou is the birthplace of tai chi chuan, and a statue of Chen Wang-din has been erected at the International College of Tai Chi in their village with the inscription describing him as the founder of the style. They denied that Jiang-fa had ever been to the Chen village, claiming that a misunderstanding arose among the people because Chen Wang-din had a guard named Jiang who was skilled in martial arts. The controversy over the beginnings of tai chi chuan is still hotly debated in China.

In 1991, an International Conference on tai chi chuan was held in Hang Dan City in North China. Delegates from the Zhaobao village in Wen County, located about two kilometers from Chenchiakou, announced in a presentation that the Zhaobao tai chi, still practiced today, was imparted by Jiang-fa, a disciple of Wang Zhong-yueh. This is a direct contradiction with the Chen family statement that the Zhaobao tai chi is a branch of the Chen-style tree. If the Zhaobao tai chi was taught by Jiang-fa, considering the close proximity of these two villages, it is reasonable to assume that Jiang-fa taught tai chi chuan in both Zhaobao and Chenchiakou.

The fact that Jiang-fa went to Chenchiakou and taught tai chi chuan to the Chen family is freely admitted by the Yang-style practitioners, whose grandmaster, Yang Lu-chan (1799–1872), spent eighteen years in Chenchiakou learning martial arts with the Chen-style master Chen Chang-hsin. Yang Lu-chan was later hired by the imperial court to teach tai chi chuan to the royal army in Beijing. He was famed for his skill in martial arts; people called him the "invincible Yang." He was the first generation of the Yang style. The second generation, his sons Yang Ban-hou (1837–1890) and Yang Jiang-hou (1842–1917), were both skilled in tai chi chuan. The third generation, the famous Yang Chen-fu, was the son of Yang Jiang-hou.

All of Yang's family acknowledged Chang San-feng as the founder of tai chi chuan. If Yang Lu-chan was the disciple of Chen Chang-hsin, and if the Chen ancestor Chen Wang-din really was the founder of tai chi chuan, then the Yang family had no reason to hide the historical facts and worship Chang San-feng as the grandmaster of tai chi chuan.

As the Chinese saying states, "He could give all the historical facts except about his own ancestor." This is not in the Chinese tradition and will continue to be criticized by many individuals. However, it is true that the Chen family was famous in martial arts for many generations, and they have enriched the martial art components of tai chi chuan with their experiences and skills.

YANG CHENG-FU AND WU CHIAN-CHUAN, CONTEMPORARY MASTERS OF THE YANG AND WU-STYLE TAI CHI CHUAN

In the early 1900s, not long after the founding of the Republic of China, Xi Yi-seng, a student of Yang Jiang-hou, founded the Athletic Research Institute in Beijing. He invited Yang Shao-hou (1862–1930) and Yang Cheng-fu (1883–1936), both the sons of Yang Jiang-hou,

FIGURE 3
Graduation picture taken in 1914 of the first tai chi chuan class of the Athletic Research Institute in Beijing. In the first seated row, the person sixth from the left is Xi Yi-seng, and the person ninth from the left is Wu Chiang-chuan. The person seated in the far-right position in the same row is believed to be the first Westerner to learn tai chi chuan in China.

FIGURE 4
Grandmaster Yang Cheng-fu in
Guangzhou (1933)

and Wu Chian-chuan, the son of Chuan Yu, to teach tai chi chuan in the Institute. This heralded a new era of allowing the public to learn tai chi chuan openly and easily. Previously, tai chi chuan was only taught to a limited group of apprentices in a traditional sifu-disciple relationship.

A picture of the graduating ceremony for the first tai chi chuan class of the Athletic Research Institute in Beijing is shown in Figure 3. It was taken in 1914. It shows an American student seated in the far right position in the first row, believed to be the first Westerner to learn tai chi chuan from China. His name was William or Williams, but little else is known about him.

As habits and lifestyles changed in the new society, both Wu Chian-chuan and Yang Cheng-fu modified their tai chi chuan, which had been passed down from their families. They omitted some of the jumping, stamping, and repetitive motions and made the forms much softer, slower, more natural, and strictly centered. It was easier to learn and much more beneficial in its health effects. Tai chi chuan originally was performed very rapidly. The fast form of the Yang style as performed by Yang Shao-hou took only three minutes, and the fast form of the

Wu style as performed by Ma Yueh-liang took only five minutes. Yang Cheng-fu's large size caused his movements to be very open, stretched out, and generous in appearance. This style of movement is apparent from pictures of his performance. The Wu style, on the other hand, is natural and precise while maintaining a strict center. In the early 1930s, both Yang Cheng-fu and Wu Chian-chuan moved from Beijing to Shanghai and popularized tai chi chuan in the southern lands of China, Ghangzhou, Hong Kong, and Macao.

From these bases, tai chi chuan eventually spread to the Western world. Today, the Yang style people are practicing is basically Yang Cheng-fu's style, and the Wu style being practiced is Wu Chian-chuan's style, although the forms often are changed considerably by the practitioners in different places.

Master Wu Chian-chuan (1870–1942) was the son of Chuan-yu, a low-ranking military officer in the Manchurian army of the Qing

FIGURE 5
Grandmaster Wu Chian-chuan in Shanghai (1940)

dynasty. Chuan-yu learned from Yang Lu-chan, who held a position in the royal army as a martial arts teacher. Yang had three students named Wan-chun, Lin-san, and Chuan-yu, whose studious ways allowed them to attain the essence of his skills. All were Manchurian, and it was said that each acquired one characteristic skill from their teacher. Respectively, these were an energetic style, an offensive style, and a neutralizing style, which were described as the muscles, bones, and skin of the human frame.

Master Wu Chian-chuan was disciplined in martial arts by his father when he was very young. His surname Wu was derived from the pronunciation of his father's Manchu name.

During the long years of practicing and teaching, he revised and enriched the tai chi chuan handed down from his family. He omitted some of the repetitions and stamping and jumping movements from the traditional forms to make them smoother and more structured. The fast form of the Wu style, on the other hand, kept the original jumping, attacking, and stamping movements.

In 1928, Master Wu Chian-chuan moved from Beijing to Shanghai to popularize Wu-style tai chi chuan. From there the art spread to the southern provinces of China, Hong Kong, Macao, and the districts of Southern Asia.

The Shanghai Chian Chuan Tai Chi Chuan Association was founded in 1932. Unfortunately, Master Wu Chian-chuan died in 1942, which marked a great loss to the world of tai chi chuan. The work of the Association was continued by Master Ma Yueh-liang, the son-in-law of Master Wu Chian-chuan. He married Master Wu Yin-hua, the daughter of Master Wu Chian-chuan, in 1930.

CHAPTER 3

The Multiple Health Benefits of Tai Chi Chuan

IT WAS EIGHT O'CLOCK on a late spring morning in 1992 when ten members of the Shanghai Chian Chuan Tai Chi Chuan Association gathered in Master Ma Yueh-liang's home to draw blood for a simple experiment. The ten subjects included the then 92-year-old Ma and the author.

Four cc's of blood were drawn from each person before and immediately after doing a 25-minute Wu-style long form. The purpose was to examine the effect of tai chi on the activating NK cell, or natural killer cell, which kills cancer cells and pathological viruses in the body. The result was encouraging: it showed that the average content of the NK cell for the ten people was significantly increased immediately after completing a set of tai chi exercises.

The experiment also allowed us to compare blood pressure before and after tai chi practice. Immediately following tai chi, all ten people's blood pressure dropped in varying degrees as compared to the blood pressures taken before the exercise that morning. Three people whose blood pressures were highest initially experienced the most significant drops. The fact that blood pressure usually drops immediately after tai chi is known to many tai chi practitioners since taking one's blood pressure is a simple procedure.

In 1986 in Hong Kong, I was the first to use the name "stillness and relaxation syndrome" to describe the state induced by practicing tai chi. The stillness and relaxation syndrome is manifested by warmth of the body, sweating, increased saliva secretion, increased peristalsis of the gastro-intestinal tract, dilation of the peripheral blood capillaries, and lowered blood pressure during the practice of tai chi. Apparently, these are signs of the increased activity of the parasympathetic nervous system. This is an important physiological basis for the health benefits of this exercise.

Stillness of the mind and relaxation of the body are interrelated. For instance, stress may cause muscle rigidity or spasm in some part of the body, which may induce low back pain or migraine. On the other hand, if some of the muscles are rigid and tense, the mind cannot be calm either. Generally, if you want to calm the body, you have to first calm the mind.

The influence of the parasympathetic activity on saliva secretion is indirect. It promotes the creation of a polypeptide in the body called bradykinin, which has the effect of dilating the peripheral blood vessels. This, in turn, promotes the secretion of saliva and sweat. Dilation of the peripheral blood capillary vessels is often evidenced by my feeling of the pulsation of these vessels in my fingertips during practice of tai chi. But the effect is by no means like switching on the button to start the machine. It depends on the quality of your exercise and the level of stillness and relaxation. To quote a famous Chinese saying, "You can reach it, but you can't get it."

Physiologically, the main differences between the parasympathetic and sympathetic nervous systems are listed as follows:

	Parasympathetic	Sympathetic
Heart rate	Decreases	Accelerates
Saliva secretion	Increases	Decreases
Intestinal peristalsis	Increases	Decreases
Peripheral vessels	Dilate	Constrict
Metabolism	Anabolism	Catabolism

For decades, I have noticed that the incidence of angina pectoris is low in those tai chi practitioners with coronary artery disease. This low incidence can be explained by the effect of the tai chi-induced stillness and relaxation reaction. My purpose is to tell the reader true stories from my own experience, and their explanation according to my own understanding. My intention in sharing these insights and cases is to arouse interest in this unique Chinese exercise, to use scientific methods and technology for further research, and to use tai chi in the prevention of various critical diseases. The following two cases illustrate the benefits of tai chi.

CASE STUDIES IN TAI CHI HEALTH

Case 1: A 50-year-old driver

A 50-year-old employee of the Shanghai Bus Company suffered from frequent episodes of chest pain for five years. Several years before the onset of the disease he was robust and healthy and had practiced the hard Shao-ling martial arts for many years.

His chest pain was characteristic of angina pectoris, with sudden onset and a feeling of tightness in the retrosternal region for a short duration (lasting only for a few minutes). The chest pain was aggravated by exertion, and precipitated by effort, emotional stress, or eating. The pain also rapidly released following the use of nitroglycerin. After several laboratory tests by hospital doctors, a diagnosis of coronary artery disease was firmly established.

The patient's symptoms were not improved despite medication over a considerable time. He had stopped his Shao-ling exercise because of chest pain during strenuous activity. He then started learning and practicing tai chi. With hard work and perseverance, the frequency of the episodes of chest pain gradually decreased within a year's training. He resumed his full work day and had no episodes of chest pain for a year or more without medication. The last electrocardiogram taken January 22, 1992, showed conspicuous improvement. About ten years after that time, when I visited Shanghai, I met him in the park and he was still doing tai chi. He was retired but engaged in a part-time job.

Case 2: A report from an American tai chi student

"I am writing you regarding the events surrounding my heart attack and the role that my study of tai chi has played in my subsequent recovery. On August 8, 1984, at the ripe old age of 41, I was visiting my mother and sister, who lived in California. At approximately 9:30 I was demonstrating a country-western line dance for them when I began to experience chest pain. I stopped dancing, and thinking the pain to be acid indigestion, I took two antacid tablets and waited for the pain to subside. Unfortunately, it only worsened, until it became a crushing pain. In ten minutes, I was convinced that I was having a heart attack. My mother and sister transported me to a local hospital, where I received all the usual diagnostic tests. I was also given nitroglycerin tablets, which helped to somewhat reduce the pain.

"After the results of my cardiac enzyme tests, the EKG indicated that I had indeed experienced a myocardial infarction. Dr. M, the cardiologist who initially treated me, gave me a treatment of TpA, or thromboplastin antecedent, to break up the clot.

"I was admitted to the hospital, where I underwent the TpA therapy. I also received other tests, including an echocardiogram. Dr. M felt that an angiogram was needed, and since the hospital I was in didn't have the facilities to do one, I was transferred to another hospital nearby. The angiogram revealed a blockage of 85 to 95 percent in an artery coming off the left anterior descending artery. Dr. M recommended that an angioplasty be done immediately.

"Unfortunately, about 20 minutes after the angioplasty was done, the artery re-occluded, and another angioplasty was necessary. After a few more days in the California hospital, I returned to Tucson, Ariz., where I made arrangements to be followed by Dr. K. Dr. K started me on a course of calcium-channel blockers, cholesterol-lowering medication, and nitroglycerin, and sent me to a cardiac rehab program. I was hospitalized in Tucson less than one month after my heart attack for unstable angina. I was relieved after a few days, but I continued to experience angina. The episodes occurred frequently, one to six times per week, and required one to four nitro tablets to relieve the pain. Dr. K placed me on a transdermal nitro patch.

"In October 1994, the pain was so severe that I was again hospitalized, and an angiogram showed the artery had re-occluded, necessitating another angioplasty. My medication was changed, substituting a beta-blocker for the calcium-channel blocker. Over the next eight months or so, I continued to experience angina regularly, even though I had modified my diet to one lower in fat and cholesterol and had begun a program of regular walking. The angina still came one to six times a week and required one to four nitro tablets to relieve the pain. On three more occasions, I was hospitalized because of the intensity of the chest pain and because of the fact that the pain was not relieved by nitroglycerin.

"I was still on the nitro patches and was back on a calcium-channel blocker at that time. My most recent hospitalization took place in May 1995. Following that hospitalization Dr. K had me talk to the nurse who ran the cardiac rehab program I had attended. She suggested I attend the tai chi classes that you were teaching. At that point I thought, "What have I got to lose?" (I was becoming quite depressed because of the continuing episodes of angina, even though I thought I was doing all the "right things" for my heart.) So, in June 1995, I began studying tai chi. Since beginning my practice of tai chi I have experienced incredible relief from the angina. I went from two to six episodes a week, with each episode requiring one to four nitro tablets to relieve the pain, to only four episodes of angina in the entire one and a half years since I began studying tai chi. And those episodes did not require nitro to relieve the pain. I am convinced that tai chi is responsible for these results. I no longer use the nitro patches, nor do I take any prescription medications—just eating right, moderate exercise, and tai chi. In addition to the relief of angina, tai chi has made me a calmer person, more centered and focused. I feel more connected to the universe and have come to the realization that I have a spiritual nature that requires nurturing in the same way my physical body requires nurturing."

Yours Sincerely,

G. B.

Angina pectoris is caused by the temporary imbalance of oxygen demand and supply to the heart muscles. The densely formed network of an immense number of arterioles, supplied by the autonomic nervous system, supplies the heart muscles. These intramyocardial arterioles demonstrate a huge capacity for dilation, and they are capable of supplying more oxygen to the heart muscles if necessary. This network may also be connected to the collateral blood vessel formation, in case one of the main epicardial arteries is blocked. Normally, the intramyocardial arterioles play an important role in regulating the blood supply to the heart muscle. Although the large epicardial coronary arteries are capable of constriction and relaxation, they serve primarily as conduits, and their capacity to control the delivery of oxygen to the heart does not compare with that of the intramyocardial arterioles.

Generally, narrowing of a coronary artery is a chronic process; some experiments indicate that the blockage can be reversed through strict diet control and exercise. Angina pectoris is induced by temporary spasm of the coronary artery. It is well-known to both doctors and the patients with coronary artery disease that physical or mental stress is the common precipitating factor of angina pectoris. According to the yin-yang theory, these factors are external, belonging to the yang, and the stillness and relaxation reaction is internal, and belongs to the yin. Any disease or pathological changes in the body can be explained by the imbalance of yin and yang, and normal physiological activities are always based on the balance of yin and yang.

WHY TAI CHI IS THE BEST BALANCE EXERCISE

In 1995 a scientific study was conducted at eight universities and medical centers about the benefits of tai chi and the prevention of falls. The medical centers at Harvard, Yale, Centers for Disease Control, Washington University School of Medicine, and Emory University all came to the conclusion that a tai chi practice program for elderly people of thirteen weeks, duration had reduced the risk of falling by 47.5 percent. This form of exercise not only improved the balance, body awareness, muscular and skeletal strength, and overall well-being, but it also contributed to the safety of an effective exercise program for the elderly. These findings were published in the *Journal of American Medical Association* in the May 3, 1995 issue. Their conclusion points out that tai chi is the only exercise that shows a significant decrease in the number of falls among the elderly, reducing the percentage of falls by almost half.

According to the article "Significance of Falls in the Elderly," published in the *American Journal of Geriatrics,* September 1996, about 30 percent of persons age 65 and older who are living at home fall each year. This rate rises to 50 percent in those over age 80. About five percent of those who fall suffer a bone fracture, resulting in 250,000 hip fractures annually in the United States. Seventy-five percent of deaths from falls occur in the elderly, even though they represent only 12 percent of the population. Although most children fall from heights, most elderly people fall on flat, level surfaces. The cost of caring for falls in the elderly has been estimated at $12.4 billion per year. Falls are also listed as a cause for 40 percent of nursing home admissions.

It is noteworthy that falls are rare among long-time tai chi practitioners. Many of the members of the Shanghai Wu-style Tai Chi Association have been over 60; the oldest was 99. Fractures and the related injuries caused by an accidental fall were never observed in the members of our Association during a fifteen-year period when I was staying in Shanghai.

The achievement of balance is evident in an accomplished tai chi master. Master Ma's demonstration of push hands was always a great attraction for many of the tai chi learners. His opponents often lost their balance and were unable to stand still at the first touch of Ma's hands. Eventually most were thrown down or fell to the ground while Ma stood calmly, looking as if he were a hardy old pine tree on the top of Yellow Mountain, standing boldly and vigorously against the blowing wind.

I have witnessed several times Master Ma's skill of *zhong-din*. He stood on one leg with the posture of the "golden cock stands on one leg." Six robust young men stood before him in a row. Each was ready to push the back of the one in front with both of their hands, while the first one applied his hands to Ma's abdomen. At the sound of a whistle, all six made a sudden push with all of their strength toward Ma's abdomen. It was amazing to see that all six were knocked back in an instant, and all were thrown to the ground. Ma was still standing on one leg; he hadn't moved an inch. He attributed this to the strength of his *zhong-din*.

The word *zhong* means "centered," and *din* "stability." *Zhong-din* is the governing principle of the thirteen kinetic movements. The other twelve are *peng, lu, ji, an, tsai, li, zhou, kao, turning to the left, turning to the right, step forward,* and *step backward;* all are based on *zhong-din.* Tai chi was called "the thirteen postures" in ancient times. *Zhong-din* is considered to be the concealed strength in tai chi, because it is barely exposed by the external movements. None of the kinetic movements can ever be dissociated from *zhong-din.* There is no fixed form or method for push hands or in real fighting, but all the forms or methods should be based on *zhong-din.*

Literally, *zhong-din* means to stabilize the center of gravity and balance the momentum. The difficulty in obtaining the strength of *zhong-din* is that all parts of the body must be suffused with internal energy. It is the combination of the mind, inner potential (qi), the eight directions, and the five basic steps as a whole.

Zhong-din has commonly been translated as "central equilibrium" in English, which denotes any condition in which all acting forces are canceled or neutralized by each other. This results in a stable, balanced system. But it describes only the mechanical function, while ignoring the important role of the mind.

Following is another true story about Master Ma. It was a late and dark evening, and Master Ma was on his way home. He stepped over the edge of an open manhole and nearly fell in. Without thinking, he suddenly changed his front leg to empty and, at the same time, shifted his body weight to his rear leg, thus saving himself from falling into the deep hole. He told us later that the situation was extremely critical and the reaction would have been too late if the response had come after "thinking." It was an automatic reflex of the mind and the body, which is created from the long-time practice of tai chi.

The changing of the empty and solid leg is one of the unique means of re-arranging the central equilibrium or *zhong-din.* It is based on the theory of yin and yang.

There are many reasons why tai chi is the best balance exercise. First, it is not only mechanical work but also an "organic" exercise. The body's balance reflex is created by the weight-bearing of the bottom of the feet, which are constantly sending nervous impulses to the spinal cord and brain. The rooting of the body weight to the bottom of the feet and the frequent changing of the empty and solid steps constantly stimulate the balance reflex center and enable its function to become more sensitive and effective.

The center of gravity is where all gravity forces from all parts of the body meet. With the legs as the support, a person can stand, but the vertical line from the center of gravity must fall within the supporting surface of the feet. If it falls outside the supporting area, one is bound to lose one's balance. Thus, the lower the center of gravity, the better the body balance will be. When practicing tai chi you have to bend the knees, sink the energy to the bottom of the abdomen, relax the muscles, and let the body weight drop according to gravity. These techniques are meant to lower your center of gravity and in turn will promote your body balance. In contrast, Western people like their "chest out," with shoulders raised and arms muscular. This results in raising their center of gravity, which may be the main cause of poor balance when they get old.

One of the causes of falls is a weakness of the legs. Tai chi strengthens the muscles of the legs and reduces the risk of a fall.

There are more mechanisms that may explain the effect of tai chi in promoting body balance—for instance, the harmony or coordination of the mind and the body. The 1995 scientific report in the *Journal of American Medical Association* (JAMA) is encouraging, especially since the experiment involved a senior group who practiced tai chi only for a thirteen-week period. What do you think the results would have been had the experiment involved a group of younger people who practiced for years?

CAN TAI CHI PREVENT OSTEOPOROSIS?

I have long noticed that the bodies of veteran tai chi practitioners always look straight and erect. Hunchback or misshapen spinal columns are rarely seen in tai chi practitioners, even when they reach 80 or 90 years of age. This was also true of Master Ma Yueh-liang when he was 98, and of Ma's wife, Master Wu Yin-hua, when she was 90.

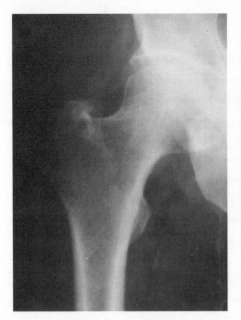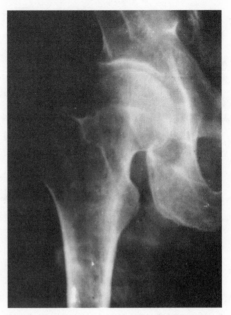

FIGURE 6

(left) The X ray film of an 83-year-old tai chi master. Notice the bone material are compact, smooth and without overt decalcification. *(right)* The X ray film of the hip joint of a 60-year-old man. He is likely to suffer a fracture should a fall occur.

An X-ray film of Master Ma's hip joint taken at the age of 83 revealed that his cortical bone mass was smooth and compact, and that there was no enlargement of the medullary cavity. In contrast, an X-ray film taken of the hip joint of a 60-year-old sedentary worker showed significant decrease of the cortical bone mass and an enlarged medullary cavity. These are the overt signs of osteoporosis by X-ray diagnosis.

The sedentary worker is likely to suffer a hip joint fracture if he ever falls. At the time the X-ray film was taken, the method of bone density scan was not commonly used to diagnose osteoporosis.

It is well known in China that Chinese martial artists usually have strong bones. Tai chi belongs to the soft internal martial arts, and it is difficult for people to understand that it is actually a unique weight-bearing exercise. Encouraged by the evidence I found in the tai chi community, I was the first to report that long-time tai chi practitioners benefit by preventing or delaying the development of osteoporosis. This was reported in a short chapter in the book *Wu-Style Push Hands,* published in Hong Kong in 1984.

Osteoporosis is the most common bone disorder in the world. In America more than 28 million people have different degrees of osteoporosis. Eighty percent are women within fifteen to twenty years following menopause. The other 20 percent experience age-related osteoporosis, and a few suffer from disease-related bone loss. According to statistics, the incidence of fracture exceeds one million per year in the United States. The majority of the victims are seniors with osteoporosis and poor body balance who are prone to fall. Fracture of the hip usually results from a fall, a common disaster of the aged.

Compression fractures of the thoracic spine are prevalent in women after menopause. Because they usually occur insidiously or silently, the exact rate of occurrence is difficult to establish. Collapse of the thoracic vertebrae results in deformity of the chest, progressive hunchback, restricted breathing, decreased body height, and acute or chronic back pain.

According to a recent survey in Beijing, the incidence of spinal fracture in 50- to 59-year-old women is 15 percent. The number increases with age and reaches 37 percent after the age of 80, which is 5.5 percent less than a similar survey carried out in the United States.

Normal stress on the bones, such as weight-bearing exercise, provides essential stimuli to the formation of the bone mass. Immobilization or no exercise leads to degenerative changes or atrophy of the bone mass due to loss of bone minerals.

Astronauts rapidly lose their bone minerals and mass when flying in space because of the effects of zero gravity; this results from no exertion to support their body and thereby retain their bone minerals. To prevent osteo-

FIGURE 7
Woman with hunchback because of spinal fracture after menopause.

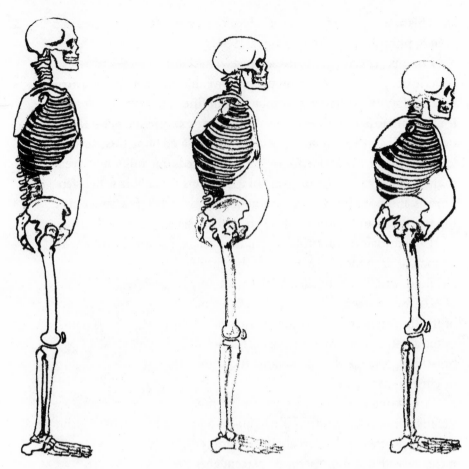

FIGURE 8
The progressive deformity of the chest because of fracture and collapse of
the thoracic vertebrae.

porosis, the astronauts must perform weight-bearing exercises while
in space.

According to clinical statistics, osteoporosis has a positive interrelationship with age: the higher the age, the higher the risk of osteoporosis. On the other hand, it has a negative interrelationship with
obesity: the heavier the body weight, the lower the risk of osteoporosis. Also, it is well-known that a thin person has a higher risk of devel-
oping osteoporosis. The most reasonable explanation is that being
obese increases the weight-bearing burden on a person's skeleton.

Weight-bearing exercise is an essential procedure in preventing osteoporosis. But many weight-bearing exercises are mainly done by stretching and contracting the muscles, thus the muscles get more exercise than the bones. The exercise of tai chi is different. Relaxation of the muscles is essential for maintaining the body's central equilibrium. This results in the bones bearing the weight of the whole body, especially the bones of the legs, hip, and spine. It is also apparent that slow and continuous movements increase the burden on the bones, because the longer the movement, the greater the acting force. The continuous use of the empty and solid step is also unique. When standing only on the solid leg, the weight-bearing will increase several-fold as compared to standing on both legs. Tai chi can be considered a true weight-bearing exercise for the bones.

One 1996 study by E. Jauer, J. Valeriano et al. entitled *Effect of tai chi on bone mineral density: A clinical investigation* examined the effect of tai chi (one hour of tai chi three times a week for six months) on bone mineral density (BMD) in fifteen healthy women (average age 52) and compared the results to a similar group of eleven women who did not perform tai chi.

The researchers found that "The tai chi group demonstrated an overall increase in total hip BMD (+1.82 percent yr.), whereas the control group decreased in total BMD by .66 percent yr., which is consistent with age-related loss."

In a different study conducted by the Weill Medical College of Cornell University in New York, it is stated that osteoporosis, which causes bone mineral deficiencies and lowers overall bone strength, can be combated by practicing tai chi. The study concurred that new methods of preventing and treating osteoporosis need to be incorporated into our current lifestyles:

> Prevention of bone loss is obviously preferable to any remedial measures, but new therapeutic strategies provide a means of restoring deficient bones."
> —*Journal of the American Academy of Orthopaedic Surgeons,* 1999

STRESS REDUCTION: THE DYNAMIC BALANCE OF YIN AND YANG

> *To rest the mind beneath the navel is to condense your spirit.*
> *To direct the qi to the abdomen beneath the navel is to*
> *   regulate the breath.*
> *The breath and the spirit correlate with each other.*
> *To maintain their purity and naturalness is termed not-to-*
> *   neglect.*
> *To follow their purity and naturalness is termed not-to-aid.*
> *With stillness and relaxation, the breath is smooth, and the*
> *   spirit is calm.*
> *Let your mind dwell in emptiness, and rest your spirit in*
> *   silence.*
> *Over and over, purify and purify, and suddenly you feel your*
> *   breath*
> *and spirit as if they did not exist. It seems that they blend*
> *   together*
> *with the whole body. You are then entranced by a spiritual*
> *   light,*
> *and intoxicated with a sense of euphoria as if you were*
> *   drunken.*
> *—from* The Collected Works of Chang San-feng

"Not-to-neglect" means the exercise should always be done with purity and naturalness. "Not-to-aid" means maintaining purity and naturalness, and avoiding self-created unnecessary thoughts or movements. To rest the mind beneath the navel is to concentrate the mind and prevent distracting thoughts.

To direct the qi to the abdomen beneath the navel is to practice abdominal breathing. This has been described as the massage of the internal organs. It may calm the mind and alleviate an acute pain.

The surface area of our diaphragm is about 300 square centimeters. When the diaphragm lowers one centimeter, you will inhale 300 cubic centimeters of air. If the diaphragm pulls down four centimeters, it means you can inhale 1,200 cubic centimeters of air. The diaphragm of a long-time tai chi practitioner usually becomes stronger and capable of moving deeper than ordinary people.

The above quotation begins with an explanation of the method of meditation, which is aimed at attaining a state of stillness. This state of stillness should not be mistaken for a suspension of the mind. On the contrary, the mind reaches its highest physiological condition. It becomes more sensitive, receptive, and adaptive, and able to transform or neutralize any outward stimulus. I have described the function of the mind as similar to water in a lake. If the water is calm, it is shining and reflects like a mirror. If it is turbulent, it can hardly reflect anything.

The commonly practiced meditation in the West involves concentrating the mind on a certain object or fixed image to prevent distracting thoughts. This, according to Taoism, is "to build the foundation," a step which is still external and intentional.

A term commonly used for meditation in China is *silent sitting*. But silent sitting is more than meditation, because its final purpose is to reach a state of stillness, which is internal and natural.

In Confucianism, silent sitting clears the mind to see the nature of life. In Buddhism, it is for seeking "the real and the eternal."

In Taoism, silently sitting is done to practice the "internal alchemy" for longevity and immortality. Although there are differences in these philosophies, religious backgrounds, and beliefs, silent sitting is the basic means of reaching a higher level of self-development and enlightenment.

To reach a state of stillness is to regain an innate ability that everybody has possessed from birth. This innate ability has been undermined or lost by our habitual behaviors. If the acquired influences are abolished, the innate functions will recover. If the absurd desires are cleared, the heavenly principles will dominate. The level of a state of stillness has no limitation. The deeper the state of stillness, the higher the function of the mind.

It is important to understand that the purpose of practicing tai chi is not to gain or create something your body has never possessed. It is to recover an innate ability with which everybody is born.

The concept of yin and yang is the dualistic principle of ancient

Chinese philosophy. As we have already discussed, everything in the universe can be separated as yin and yang. The two are opposite and complementary. Without one the other will not exist. For instance, without cold you can never understand warm; without worry you could not experience happiness; and with no death life becomes meaningless.

Life can be defined as a series of constant reactions to the external and internal stimuli of the body, which ultimately ends with death.

Stress is the yang. It is the everlasting initiator, and also the motivating force.

The yin, as explained in the *Book of Changes*, is silence and stillness, but it constantly moves and changes by the influence of the yang. Absolute stillness never exists. Interestingly, the sun in Chinese is called *tai yang*, which means "the greatest yang."

It is apparent that without stress there will be no change and creation in life. Actually, without stress there will be no human life at all.

Since the same stress may create different responses in different individuals, managing stress depends largely upon one's state of mind. Humans create two different kinds of thoughts. One is the "real thoughts," which follow the rule of Nature; for instance, if you are hungry you have to eat. The other is the "absurd thoughts," which usually spring from a private desire for control and lead to stress.

If the rules of Nature can gain control of your private desires, you survive. If absurd desires prevail over the rules of Nature, you court destruction.

Remember, stress is the outward stimuli, which is the constant initiator. It is the yang. The role of human life is to neutralize or adapt to these endless encounters. It is the yin. Normal physiological and mental activities depend on the dynamic balance of the yin and yang.

CHAPTER 4

The Fundamentals of Tai Chi Chuan

Never neglect the roles of the head, waist, stance, and torso;
Lacking any of these your effort will be to no avail.
If you ignore the roles of any of these essentials,
You will be muddled even after ten years of practice.
—from the book *On the Essence of Tai Chi*,
The author is unknown.

THE IMPORTANCE OF WARDING FORCE (PENG)

The warding force (peng) ranks to the first of the eight kinetic movements, namely warding, diverting, pressing, pushing, plucking, twisting, elbowing and leaning. The first four are often named the four frontal methods, and the last four the diagonal hands methods.

The warding force is considered to be the hidden strength because it is not exposed in the external movements. In push hands any part of the body that connects with the opponent should apply the warding force, no matter if it is the hand, arm, shoulder, back, or any part of the body.

Actually, the warding force is created from the long time practicing of the forms, which stands for "no resist" and "no escape" but always to stick and follow the offensive force from the enemy. The warding force is relatively hard to learn for beginners. Only when the student learned the nature of the warding force, may he be considered to have acquired the rudiments of push hands. In the 1950s, some of the well-known masters in Shanghai, such as Ku Liu-xin and Tiang

Shao-lin, stated in their book or articles that the martial arts of tai chi chuan can be considered as the martial arts of warding force.

The article, *The Mechanics of Eight Kinetic Movements,* by the late tai chi master Wu Gong-tsao, the youngest son of the grandmaster Wu Chian-chuan, says, "that the warding force is like adding a band on the geared wheel, the effect is to decrease its intensity, change its direction, and prevent the opponent's force from reaching your own body, whether the oncoming force is strong or weak, fast or slow."

With the warding force you are able to have what the classic says "rapid response for rapid attacking" and "slow response for slow offensive." The so-called *tin jin* or the audible force is actually based on the warding force.

The Classic also says, "If the opponent doesn't move, I don't move. If the opponent starts to move, I move beforehand." This effect can hardly be achieved without applying your warding force.

Indeed, the warding force may be described as the water in the ocean. It drifts a tiny leaf, but it can also carry a ten-thousand-ton boat. The difference is that the boat is floated by the buoyancy of the water, while the warding force is mainly created by skill.

The warding force is also called the supporting force by some of the authors. The main role of the warding force is to control the direction of the opponent's attacking force, and prevent it from reaching your body.

The warding force should never exceed the opponent's attacking force. When the opponent attacks, his momentum and inertia carry him forwards. It requires much less strength to change his direction. Much like riding on a running bicycle, the direction of the front wheel changes easily just by slightly turning the handle bars.

Regretfully, the warding force is often misinterpreted by many of the tai chi practitioners. Since any part of the body which makes contact with the opponent should apply the warding force, it has no fixed direction. During push hands the opponent usually attacks in the front. It is natural that your warding force should be upward and backward. The effect of the upward and backward strength is to allow the opponent to advance, but prevent him reaching your own body. If the oncoming force is in the front, and your warding force is upward and forward, it can only create the resisting force, which contradicts the basic rule "not to resist and not to escape."

In most of such instances, the opponent will be frustrated or become impatient and would likely launch a sudden attack with his full strength. This may create what the Classic describes as the "favorable time and condition" for you to make a successful counterattack.

We name the warding force as the living force or organic. It requires a high level of skill, which can be accomplished only through long time practice of push hands and the long form. We call the simple, mechanical movements, the "dead force." It is hard for those who have never done push hands or those without the basic skill of the forms, to understand even after much explanation.

I once heard from the late grandmaster Ma Yueh-liang that the real comprehension of any higher level to have been reached only when the student has reached such level through practice. Otherwise, you are still confused.

THE CORRECT BODY POSTURES
AND ALIGNMENT

The Head

Keeping the head erect and the neck empty, or *hui-lin-din-jin* in Chinese, is of prime importance in practicing the forms of tai chi. When standing, let the body weight, from the shoulders to the legs, drop naturally according to the Earth's gravity. Keep the head erect, as if the top of the head were pulled up by a string from the heavens.
The neck in turn supports the head, but its muscles are relaxed, using the sense, not force.

For most people, the chin normally stands out slightly below the mouth. According to Master Ma Yueh-liang , it should be drawn back about three or four centimeters. The effect is to straighten the neck and the head, and to enhance the propping force at the top of the head. The method is termed *din jin*, one of the special nomenclatures of tai chi. The word *din* means "propping" and *jin* is "strength."

By drawing the chin a little bit inward, the eyes will naturally look slightly downward and form about a 25-degree angle to the surface of the ground about 20 feet from your toes. If the eyes look upward, like a soldier standing at attention, your neck is bent considerably. Your neck is still bent forward even if you are looking horizontally to the front.

The main effects of *hui-lin-din-jin* are three-fold. First, it raises your spirit. If you look in the mirror with an erect head, you will find yourself looking more energetic and with higher spirit. As the Classic states,

> The so-called suspending the top of the head has the effect of promoting the spirit and prevents one from being heavy and clumsy.
> —*Key to the Thirteen Kinetic Movements*

> The coccyx is centered, and the spirit raised to the top of the head, Your body will be light and agile while the top is suspended.
> —*Chant of the Thirteen Kinetic Movements*

Second, it creates the opposing strength of the body in a vertical position. "Opposing strength" refers to the two strengths that pull each other from opposite directions, which results in the elongation of the muscles or the tendons of the joint. The role of the opposing force is to stabilize the center of gravity and balance the momentum.

When one is standing, the energy of the head goes upward to the heavens, while the weight of the remaining parts of the body sink to the earth. They pull against each other in an opposite and vertical direction.

Opposing strength is one of the unique features of tai chi, and not only in the vertical position; almost all of the movements include the effects of the opposing strength.

Third, *hui-lin-din-jin* is connected with other essential features of tai chi. For instance, it straightens the spinal column. Without *hui-lin-din-jin* there would be no centered tailbone.

With *hang-shun-ba-bei*, which means loosening the chest and lifting the back, it is apparent that the back can be lifted only by *hui-lin-din-jin;* there is no other way to lift the back.

The eyes represent the intention of the mind. The eyesight should be calm and natural, while following the main direction of the movement. The eyes should never be closed with any movement.

The Waist

The Chinese concept of the waist includes the narrow part of the trunk between the chest and the hips, as well as the two soft lateral sides and the two large paraspinal muscles in the back. The front part of the abdomen is usually excluded. The two soft sides are not protected by bones and are vulnerable to attack. The center of the back of the waist, called *min men,* or "life gate," plays an important role in tai chi.

It is commonly said that tai chi uses the mind rather than force. But to say that tai chi has no force or never uses force is wrong. The following verse of the Classics explains how the force is created:

> The energy of tai chi is rooted in the feet,
> Transmitted through the legs,
> Dominated by the waist,
> And figured in the hands.

While tai chi contains tremendous force, it is usually not necessary to use this force. A common saying is that tai chi borrows the force from the earth. When you stand, the acting force sinks into the ground, but at the same time the earth creates a reacting force, which allows your body to be balanced and stay upright. Because the whole body, including the mind, works together as one entity, the sinking force can be increased immensely, especially when you are using the hard or rigid resistance from the body of an opponent.

The sinking of the strength is referred to as *chen jin,* another special term of tai chi. The word *chen* means "sink" and *jin* is "strength." This reacting force from the ground can be transmitted through your legs, waist, arms, and hands, to finally reach the body of your opponent. The case is much like a car running into a wall; the rebounding force will send the car backward. The faster the speed of the car, the stronger the rebound force. These acting and counteracting forces have no limits, as the ancient Greek giant Hercules pointed out when he said he could hold up the Earth if he could get support for his legs.

The waist is the axis and plays an important role. Most of the Western learners of tai chi are not accustomed to using their waists. When people exercise on machines, they are incessantly doing pulling and stamping work with their extremities. They scarcely use the mind to direct the movements. They neglect the important roles of the mind and waist. Although their arms and legs can become muscular and strong, the waist usually is stiff. When they make turns, they turn the upper body first and the waist follows. Sometimes they even turn the whole body together. With tai chi, the waist is the *banner*, the axis, and is the leading force that directs other parts of the body's movements. Most of the tai chi forms, such as the *opening* and *closing, ascending* and *sinking,* are made mainly by the waist.

To quote a saying from a Classic,

> Never neglect any of the thirteen kinetic movements,
> And remember the waist is the source of sense and
> perception.
> —*Chant of the Thirteen Kinetic Movements*

The area of *min men,* the "life gate," is located at the middle portion of the back of the waist. This is the critical area when you are projecting energy. The *min men* should protrude backward when you are making a punch or push. In brush knee and twist step, when the palm pushes to the front, the *min men* draws backward at the same time. This can be shown when shooting an arrow; the bow string should be pulled backward to send the arrow forward.

Moving the waist backward when projecting the energy to the front also creates the opposing strength. This is often difficult to do for many Western students. Protrusion of the chest forward, bending of the waist inward, and protrusion of the buttocks outward have now become the Western style of body alignment. This posture increases the curvatures of the spine, mainly in the waist region, and may be the cause of much intractable low back pain.

The Stance

The stance, according to the Classics, involves the shape of the whole-body movements.

Despite the variations of the postures, all the movements in tai chi are based on *zhong-din*. The word *zhong* means "centered" and *din* means "stability." The centered stability implies that all parts of the body, mentally and physically, are balanced naturally according to the theory of yin and yang. There are differences between *zhong-din* and balance. *Zhong-din* is Nature's way, while balance can be created intentionally, such as by using the body's own strength, being supported by a cane, or leaning on the wall. *Zhong din* is also not the same as central equilibrium. The latter is the condition of a system in which the result of all forces is equal to zero. This can be reached through intentionally mechanical work. The point of issue is that *zhong-din* is controlled by the mind. The Classics describe it as follows:

> It is the mind and spirit that are the master,
> And the bones and muscles are the servant.
> —*Chant of the Thirteen Kinetic Movements*

There are no fixed forms to be used in push hands or a real fighting, but any movement of tai chi should be based on *zhong-din*.

The difficulty in learning *zhong-din* is that all parts of the body need to be suffused with internal energy. It can be defined as the combination of the mind, inner potential, the *eight directions,* and the *five steps* working together as a whole. The skill of *zhong-din* is an important criterion in evaluating one's level of tai chi forms or push hands.

The differentiation of empty and solid is another unique feature of tai chi. Every movement has its empty and solid aspects, and every part of the body contains the effects of empty and solid. As for taking a step, the empty leg is the yin and the solid leg is the yang. Yin and yang are constantly moving and changing, and they represent the unity of the opposites, because without one the other will not exist.

The movement of the legs or arms without the differentiation of empty and solid, or yin and yang, is called *double weighting*. This is a common and serious mistake in practice that should always be prevented.

In the typical stance of the Wu-style archery step, the body is inclined forward, forming a 20- or 25-degree angle with the ground. The back of the head, the back, the rear leg, and the heel form a straight line. The front leg is solid and the rear leg is empty. Experience confirms that this posture is most advantageous for sending energy and also maintaining body balance.

It is apparent that with the archery step, if the upper body is erect, the waist will be bent and the spine and tailbone will not be in a straight line.

The Torso

"Torso" usually denotes the trunk, which excludes the head and limbs. But since the energy of tai chi is created through the integration of the whole body, the roles of the torso can't be separated from other parts of the body—namely the head and extremities.

There is a common saying in tai chi:

> Tai chi is not only using the hands,
> Any part of the body can be the hand.

Any part of the torso, such as the arms and legs, can be used for diverting, attacking, or neutralizing, and contains the empty and solid aspects. The methods of using the torso are called *shen fa*. The word *shen* means "body," and *fa* is the "methods."

Following is another story about Master Ma. He was teaching a morning class on the bank of the Whangpu River of Shanghai, and there was a student who always fell to the ground or could not control his balance when he was learning push hands with Ma. This student thought of a plan to test Ma's skill with a sneak attack. He suddenly grasped Ma's body with both arms from the back with all his might when Ma was walking to class at the waterfront. No sooner had the student cried out, "Now I have you!" than he was thrown back into a small tree near the sidewalk. The tree broke under the weight.

Ma was wearing a linen gown, which had just been ironed. He stood peacefully, turned back, and said to the student, "What are you doing with me? Look! My gown is all crumpled!"

I once asked Master Ma what I should do if someone grasped me tightly from behind. He wanted me to make an attempt on him. I grasped his body from the back and used all my energy with both arms. I immediately felt every muscle in his body shake, as if I had just grabbed the body of a tiger. I loosened my hands and drew back. Yes, I was frightened! My fellow student told me later that my face suddenly turned pale.

Sinking the energy to the *dan tian* is another essential in practicing tai chi. The *dan tian* is the area about two inches below the umbilicus where the body's center of gravity is usually located. Sinking the energy to the *dan tian* with *empty neck* and *erect head* creates opposing strength and straightens the torso.

Sinking the energy to the dan tian should be made natural. It is using the mind rather than force.

The breathing should be slow, even, deep, and natural. Avoid using force. Breathing can follow the tempo of the movements, but because of the variations of the time or duration of the movements, breathing can't match the movements. In fact, breathing in tai chi is an inseparable part of the whole-body movement.

To sink the energy to the *dan tian* is also to practice the abdominal breathing. When you *fa jin,* which means "issue the energy with a sudden punch or push," you breath out. But at the same time, the diaphragm pushes downward. This is called reversed abdominal breathing, the effect of which is increasing the body's opposing strength.

Another principle of tai chi taught by the Classics is that force is issued from the back of the spine, which is termed *li you ji fa.* This means the energy is issued from your back. The practitioner should understand that although the strength is rooted in the feet and transmitted through the legs, a strong back is still the best support for launching strength. This is especially true when the muscles in other parts of the body are relaxed.

Relaxation of the muscles and mind is called *soong,* another special term often used in tai chi. *Soong* is by no means a slackening of the body and mind. *Soong* helps the mind and muscles be more sensitive and flexible, while allowing the internal energy to be circulated smoothly to any part of the body according to the will power of the mind.

CHAPTER 5

The Solo Form: The Authentic Method of the Wu-Style Slow Form

Tai chi can be divided into two main systems—form and application. The form includes the methods or movements, in which all parts of the body, including the mind, breathing, internal energy, as well as the body structure and appearance, coordinate or work together according to the mind's intention. The mind directs the energy and the energy directs the movements. Although tai chi is often taught in classes or practiced in groups, self-practice is essential for cultivating internal energy and personal enlightenment. Hence the name solo form or one-man tai chi.

Push hands has been called two-man tai chi, because you need a partner. The two people compete or fight with each other with fixed steps or moving steps based on the methods and spirit learned from the forms.

Push hands is said to be the explanation of the forms. Through push hands, the player may test his tai chi skills or discover incorrect movements in his forms.

Tai chi is the integration of the mind, energy, and body. Any single movement is a part of the whole-body movement; and if any single part of the body stops moving, all parts of the body stop at the same time. It is an organic whole. It seems that simple mechanical work, such as exercise on a machine, is exercise for exercise's sake, while tai chi is exercise for your whole being.

The slow and continuous motions prolong the duration of the movements; the longer the acting time, the more energy you require. The slow movements also help you enjoy the inner feelings. It is much like eating; by eating rapidly, you can hardly enjoy the real taste of the food.

The chemical changes in the body after performing tai chi also differ from those involving heavy and strenuous exercises. Usually a tai chi practitioner feels high-spirited and energetic, ready to continue the movements after completing a 25-minute form. The effects can be explained by the stillness and relaxation reaction, as well as by a decreased accumulation and accelerated removal of lactic acid because of the slow, low-impact movements.

A slow set may take about 20 to 25 minutes to complete. However, that number can climb to 30 to 60 minutes. No matter how slow your practice, the movement must be continuous and even. As the Classics describe, it is like pulling silk from a cocoon. The internal energy should flow smoothly with the movements.

Breaking or interrupting the flow of any movement is termed *duan jin*. The word *duan* means "break" and *jin* is "strength." *Duan jin* is a common mistake in tai chi, especially when it comes to push hands. The continuing or flowing movement can always change if an external force is encountered. But when the movement stops an attack is likely. A break in the movements also stops the flow of internal energy. There are 89 forms in the Wu-style tai chi set, including the preparation and closing forms. If the 49 repetitions are excluded, the number of the basic forms is only 38. Following are the names and sequence of the forms:

1. The Preparation Style
2. The Beginning Form
3. Grasping The Bird's Tail
4. Single Whip
5. Raise Hand and Step Up
6. White Stork Flaps Its Wings
7. Brush Knee and Twist Step
8. Hand Strums The Lute
9. Step Up, Diverting and Blocking Punch
10. As If Closing Up
11. Tiger and Leopard Spring to the Mountain
12. Cross Hands
13. Oblique Brush Knee Twist Step

14. Turn Body, Oblique Brush Knee and Twist Step
15. Grasping the Bird's Tail
16. Oblique Single Whip
17. Fist Under Elbow
18. Repulse Monkey
19. Flying Oblique
20. Raise Hands and Step Up
21. White Stork Flaps Its Wings
22. Brush Knee Twist Step
23. Needle at the Bottom of the Sea
24. Fan Through the Back
25. Parry and Punch
26. Move Back, Diverting and Blocking Punch
27. Step Up, Grasping the Bird's Tail
28. Single Whip
29. Cloud Hands
30. Single Whip
31. High Pat the Horse
32. Left and Right Parting Leg
33. Turn Body, Pedaling Foot
34. Step Up, Planting Punch
35. Turn Body, Parry and Punch
36. Step Up, Parry and Punch
37. Open Body and Kick
38. Retreat Step, Beat the Tiger
39. Strike the Ears with Double Fists
40. Turn Body, Double Kicking
41. High Pat the Horse
42. Step Up, Diverting and Blocking Punch
43. As If Closing Up
44. Tiger and Leopard Spring to the Mountain
45. Cross Hands
46. Oblique Brush Knee and Twist Step
47. Turn Body, Oblique Brush Knee and Twist Step
48. Grasping the Bird's Tail
49. Oblique Single Whip

50. Parting the Wild Horse's Mane
51. Jade Girl Works at the Shuttle
52. Grasping the Bird's Tail
53. Single Whip
54. Cloud Hands
55. Single Whip
56. Downward Posture
57. Golden Cockerel Standing on One Leg
58. Repulse Monkey
59. Flying Oblique
60. Raise Hand and Step Up
61. White Stork Flaps Its Wings
62. Brush Knee Twist Step
63. Needle at the Bottom of the Sea
64. Fan Through the Back
65. Parry and Punch
66. Step Up, Diverting and Blocking Punch
67. Step Forward, Grasping the Bird's Tail
68. Single Whip
69. Cloud Hands
70. Single Whip
71. High Pat the Horse
72. Palm to Meet the Face
73. Turn Body, Cross Swinging Lotus
74. Pointing to the Crotch Punch
75. Step Up, Grasping the Bird's Tail
76. Single Whip
77. Downward Posture
78. Step Up to Form the Seven Star
79. Retreat Step, Ride the Tiger
80. Turn Body, Hit the Face Palm
81. Turn Body, Double Swinging Lotus
82. Curve Bow, Shoot Tiger
83. Step Up, High Pat the Horse
84. Palm to Meet the Face
85. Turn Body, Parry and Punch

86. Step Up, High Pat the Horse
87. Step Up, Grasping the Bird's Tail
88. Single Whip
89. Closing Tai Chi

The above forms can be divided into the following six sections. Notice that each section ends with single whip.

Section one—From preparation method to oblique single whip. 16 forms.
Section two—From fist under elbow to single whip. Form 17 to 30.
Section three—From high pat the horse to oblique single whip. Forms 31 to 49.
Section four—From parting the wild horse's mane to single whip. Forms 50 to 55.
Section five—From downward posture to single whip. Forms 56 to 70.
Section six—From high pat the horse to closing tai chi. Forms 71 to 89.

THE DIRECTION DIAGRAM

Tai chi practioners usually face south when starting to practice the forms. According to the belief of the ancient Chinese, the south is the yang, representing brightness, power, and warmth. This is why all the imperial buildings in Beijing were built facing south. It is by no means the unchangeable rule. You may face any direction in which you feel comfortable and which is convenient. However, for avoiding confusion and wrong movements, beginners are often advised to face the same direction when starting to practice the forms.

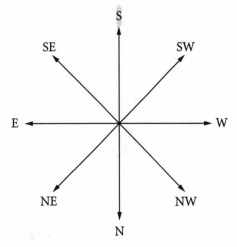

There are four different degrees of the turnings. From the south to the south-east is the 45-degree turning; from the south to the east or west is the 90-degree turning; from the south-east to the north-west is the 180-degree turning; from the east to the east in a circle is the 360-degree turning.

The entire set of the Wu-style slow form returns exactly to the starting point if the steps and the turnings are made precisely according to the five basic steps.

EXPLANATIONS OF THE SELECTED POSTURES OF THE SLOW FORM

1. The Preparation Style

Stand upright, facing south. Draw the chin a little bit inward, so the head is erect and the eyes will naturally look slightly downward *(hui-lin-din-jin)*. Loosen the chest and lift the back up by the neck (hang-shun-ba-bei). The spine and the tailbone are straight. Sink the energy to the *dan tian (qi-chen-dan-tian)*. The shoulders are dropped and the elbows hang to the sides of the body. The hands are relaxed with the fingers pointing downward. The knees are slightly bent, but the muscles of the legs should be relaxed. The feet are parallel, separated by the distance of one transverse foot, with the toes pointing to the front. The whole body weight is concentrated at the bottom of the feet, as if rooted in the earth.

FIGURE 1

Gradually raise the arms upward and forward to the level of the shoulders. The shoulders and the muscles of the arms are loose and the elbows pointed slightly downward. The fingers are slightly separated and the palms face downward. The movement should be slow, even, continuous, and without force, which has been described as pulling silk from a cocoon.

After the arms are raised to shoulder level, without breaking the flowing energy bend the elbows and drop the arms to the sides of the body with the palms bending up. This ends the preparation method.

FIGURE 2

2. The Beginning Form

From the preparation style move the left foot two feet to the front, with the heel lightly touching the ground and the toes pointing upward. The right leg is bent and all the body weight is on the right leg. This is called the empty step. The left leg is empty and belongs to yin; the right leg is solid and belongs to yang. At the same time both arms circle to the front. The left palm is transverse, facing inward, with the right thumb in line with the nose. The right palm is vertical, placed behind the left palm at the level of the curve of the left elbow.

FIGURE 3

3. Grasping the Bird's Tail

From the beginning form pivot the left foot on its heel and the right foot on its toes to the right, forming the right empty step. The body turns to the west. The right hand is about one foot away from the face, with the thumb in line with the nose and the palm facing left. The left fingers are touching the right wrist. The fingers are straight, but the muscles are loose. The elbows are pointing slightly downward. This is called the erect palm method, and it contains important martial arts functions. It is also called "playing the *pi ba*" hand. *Pi ba* is a traditional Chinese musical instrument. See Figure 4.

4. Grasping the Bird's Tail

Move the body slightly backward and turn the right palm to face upward; then, without breaking the flow, turn the body to the south-

FIGURE 4

west. At the same time shift the body weight to the front, forming the right archery step, in which the right foot is solid and the left is empty.

With the left fingers touching the right wrist, turn the body from the left to the right in a curve until the arms and the body turn to the northwest. Then, without breaking the flow, move the arms and body backward, form the empty step, and resume the posture as in Figure 4.

Notice three key points in performing grasping the bird's tail. First, when you are moving from the empty step to the archery step or from the archery step to the empty step, you are moving the whole body. The body moves first and the step follows. Second, the turning is made by the waist; the waist turns first, and the extremities follow. Third, notice the role of the opposing force or the stretching; when the arms stretch to the front, the body weight sinks downward through the solid leg.

Grasping the bird's tail is a basic tai chi method. There are nine repetitions in a long-form set, which shows its importance. It comprises the four basic techniques of push hands—warding, diverting, pressing, and pushing.

5. Single Whip

From the posture in Figure 4, turn the body to the southwest. The right palm pushes in the same direction, with the left fingers touching the right wrist. The height of the right palm is in line with the nose. Both elbows are bent. At the same time, pivot the right heel to the left to form the right "T" step. Then move the left foot about two feet leftward and about a half-foot backward. The body is slightly inclined to the front and the feet are parallel.

FIGURE 5A   FIGURE 5B

6. Single Whip

Stand with the horseback riding posture, facing slightly to the southeast. The torso is straight and centered, as if it were sitting on a bench.

Figure 6

Both arms are slightly bent. The right palm is bent, with the five fingers gathering at one point and forming the hook hand. The left palm is pushing to the southeast, and the eyes are looking at the back of the left palm. The height of the left palm is in line with the nose.

The crotch should be round, as if both thighs were wrapped around a big ball in front of the body. The *min men* should protrude out, and the buttocks pull inward.

The legs are separated about two feet from each other, with both feet pointing symmetrically and slightly to the outside.

Single whip is another main posture of tai chi, in addition to its martial arts function. It promotes body balance. The torso is like an erect pole, and the two arms and two legs are like four ropes that pull each other from different directions to stabilize the body. There are eleven repetitions in a set of Wu-style tai chi.

7. Raise Hand and Step Up

From single whip, shift the body weight to the left foot and turn the left palm upward. At the same time, lean the left shoulder leftward and

FIGURE 7

slightly backward. Open the right hook hand and push the right palm downward to the right. The eyes look at the back of the right palm.

8. Raise Hand and Step Up

From the preceding posture, draw the right foot a half-step to the front, forming the right empty step. At the same time, circle both arms to the front of the chest. The right palm is transverse,

FIGURE 8

facing inward, and the left palm is vertical, facing outward. Then bend the right knee, forming the right archery step. The body is inclined to the front and the eyes look slightly downward.

FIGURE 9

9. Raise Hand and Step Up

Straighten the waist and draw the left foot forward, forming the parallel step with the right foot. At the same time, gradually turn the right palm upward about one fist distance from the top of the forehead. The fingers are straight and the palm facing upward. The left arm is at the side of the left hip, and the left palm is bent and pushing downward. The fingers point to the front. The body is straight, the knees are slightly bent, and the eyes look slightly downward.

10. White Stork Flaps Its Wings

From the preceding posture, bend the upper body to the front. The right palm keeps one fist distance above the forehead, and the left arm naturally stretches out slightly to the front. With the feet unchanged and the knees slightly bent, gradually turn the waist to the east. The head is also turned to the east, and the eyes follow the direction of the right palm. During the turning, the right palm keeps its position at the top of the forehead. The distance between the two palms is fixed.

FIGURE 10

FIGURE 11

11. White Stork Flaps Its Wings

Gradually straighten the waist and raise the left arm to the level of the left shoulder. Then turn the waist gradually toward due south. At the same time, the right arm also moves to the front. Both arms are slightly bent, and the elbows are placed at the level of the shoulders. The hands are raised slightly above the head, with the palms facing forward and inward, much like holding a basketball. The eyes look forward and slightly downward. The step is not changed.

12. Brush Knee and Twist Step

From the previous posture the body has turned 90 degrees to the left, facing east.

Draw the right palm backward, with the right elbow pointing downward. The right palm is raised to ear level, with the fingers pointing to the front. Drop the left palm and draw it across the left knee with a round movement—hence the term "brush knee." The body is still in left empty step; the eyes look to the front.

FIGURE 12

FIGURE 13

13. Brush Knee and Twist Step

This is the first of the three successive brush knee and twist steps. The body is inclined to the front, forming the left archery step. The right palm is pushing to the east with the right index finger in line with the nose. The right arm is slightly bent, and the right elbow is pointing downward. The left palm is pushing downward at the side of the left hip. The two arms move in different directions, creating opposing forces. The eyes look at the back of the right palm.

14. Brush Knee and Twist Step

From the preceding posture move the right foot inward and forward to the right side of the left foot. Then, without a breaking of strength, the right foot continues to move forward in a curve and forms the right archery step—hence the term "twist step."

FIGURE 14

Sometimes this is also called the cat step, because the shape of the continuing twist step looks much like a cat walking. The left palm simultaneously pushes to the front and the right palm pushes downward at the right side of the hip.

With the right archery step, the left palm pushes to the front; with the left archery step, the right palm pushes to the front. The palms create the balanced opposing forces.

15. Hand Strums the Lute

FIGURE 15

The position comes directly from brush knee and twist step. Standing with parallel step, the body is upright and facing east. The right arm is dropped to the right side of the body. The right forearm is bent to the front, forming a right angle with the upper arm. The right palm faces upward with the fingers pointing to the front. The left hand forms the erect palm, facing east, and is placed at the middle portion of the body in front of the chest. The eyes look to the front. The point is that the energy of the left palm goes forward, while that of the right palm goes backward. They are balanced but contain the effect of the opposing force.

16. Step Up, Diverting and Blocking Punch

From the previous posture, stretch the left leg to the front and form the left empty step. At the same time draw the left palm to the top of the

FIGURE 16

right hand and form the high-pat-the-horse-hands (the method of high-pat-the-horse-hands will be explained later). Draw the body to the front to form the left archery step. Both palms are stretched to the front. Then draw the body backward and resume the left empty step; the body weight is concentrated on the right leg. The right palm forms a fist. Draw it back along the left forearm and rest it at the right side of the hip. The left palm still stretches to the front. This is the method of diverting.

17. Step Up, Diverting and Blocking Punch

From the previous posture, shift the body weight to the front to form the left archery step. At the same time make a punch with the right

FIGURE 17

fist to the front at the center and shoulder level. The right hand forms the erect fist, which means that the angle formed by the thumb and index finger, usually called *hu kou* in Chinese, is facing upward. The left palm rests at the curve of the right elbow.

This is the unique punch method used in tai chi. Moving the body from empty step to archery step while using the strength of the waist greatly increases the power of the punch. The left leg can also be used to block the enemy's right leg and prevent him from retreating or escaping.

18. As If Closing Up

From the previous posture draw the left palm around the right elbow to the right and facing inward. At the same time open the right fist,

FIGURE 18

then draw the right palm forward and the left palm backward until both palms are crossed in front of the chest.

Then turn both arms inward. At the same time gradually draw the body backward; the left empty step is changed into right archery step. The palms are shoulder-width apart, facing inward, and the fingers are level with the shoulders. The eyes look slightly downward through the middle space of the palms.

FIGURE 19

19. Tiger and Leopard Spring to the Mountain

From the previous posture turn both palms to the front. At the same time gradually shift the body weight to the front and resume the left archery step. The palms are pushed to the front by the waist, first slightly downward, then upward. The elbows are pointing downward. The height of the wrists is level with the shoulders; the eyes are looking at the palms.

20. Tiger and Leopard Spring to the Mountain

From the previous posture drop the elbows. The palms are pushed downward to the sides of the left knee. The palms are bent and the fingers point to the front. The body is inclined about 70 degrees to the front, but the back of the body should be straight.

FIGURE 20

The methods of as if closing up and tiger and leopard spring to the mountain are sequential movements. Using the hands for diverting or attacking without the differentiations of yin and yang is seldom advisable in tai chi. The waist plays an important role whether you are diverting or attacking.

The name "tiger and leopard spring to the mountain" was passed down by the late grandmaster Wu Chian-chuan, based on the graphic character of the forms. Variations of the names are used by different teachers.

FIGURE 21

21. Cross Hands

From the previous posture turn both palms upward, then part the left arm to the left and the right arm to the right. At the same time pivot the heels of the left and right foot to the south, forming the parallel step facing south. The palms are crossed at shoulder level in front of the chest. The right palm is placed in front of the left palm. The fingers are straight. The eyes look to the front.

This is one of the closing methods of tai chi. The parallel step is the *zhong- din* style; you can turn the body either left or right according to the direction of the attacking force.

22. Oblique Brush Knee and Twist Step

From the previous posture, turn the body 45 degrees to the southeast and form the left archery step. At the same time drop the left palm to the left side of the hip and push the right palm

FIGURE 22

to the southeast, with the right index finger in line with the nose.

If the force of the opponent comes from the southeast, you can divert it with your left hand and strike back with your right palm. The mechanism is the same with brush knee and twist step.

Figure 23

23. Turn Body, Oblique Brush Knee and Twist Step

This is a 180-degree turn. From the previous posture raise the left palm to the level of the left ear. Drop the right palm to the left side of the abdomen facing downward. At the same time turn the waist to the right and backward. After turning the body, both of the legs pivot on the heels to the right. The weight is on the left foot.

24. Turn Body, Oblique Brush Knee and Twist Step

From the previous posture, turn the waist to the northwest. The right foot now moves in the same direction as the

Figure 24

body. At the same time, pivot the left foot on its heel to the northwest. Then bend the right knee to form the right archery step. The body weight is shifted to the right leg. The left palm is pushed in the same direction to the front of the body, with the left index finger in line with the nose. The right palm brushes through the front of the right knee and pushes downward at the side of the right hip. The body is inclined 70 degrees to the front; the eyes look at the back of the left palm.

The method has strong martial arts functions. The left foot is the axis, and the centrifugal force from the body turn can overthrow the opponent.

25. Oblique Single Whip

This is the first repetition of the form single whip; only in this case does one face the southwest. The body is straight and centered, as if sitting on a bench. The eyes are looking at the back of the left palm. This is the end of the first section.

FIGURE 25

26. Fist Under Elbow

From the previous posture, open the right claw hand with the right palm facing downward. Pivot the left foot on its heel to the east. Bend the left knee to the front and shift the body weight to the left leg. At the same time move the right leg to the right, with the toes pointing east. This forms the left archery step. The arms are stretched out, with the left fingers pointing to the front and right fingers pointing to the back. The eyes look at the left palm.

FIGURE 26

FIGURE 27

27. Fist Under Elbow

From the previous posture, continue to draw the right palm to the front and place it under the wrist of the left palm. The body faces the front, and the left archery stance remains unchanged. The eyes look to the front.

28. Fist Under Elbow

Draw the body and the left foot backward. The left archery step changes to a left empty step. At the same time gradually change the right palm and the left palm into fists. Bend the left elbow and draw the left fist inward to the distance of about one foot from the mouth, with the *hu kou* (the surface of the angle formed at the root of the thumb and index finger) facing the mouth. The right fist moves along the bottom of the left forearm to the tip of the left elbow, with the *hu kou* facing upward. The body weight is sitting on the right leg; the eyes look to the front.

FIGURE 28

FIGURE 29

29. Repulse Monkey

From the previous posture, change the left fist into palm facing upward. Turn the waist to the southeast. The left palm and fingers follow the body turning. Then without breaking the strength, turn the waist to the northeast. The left palm follows the body turning and is still facing upward. At the same time, shift the body weight to the front and resume the left archery step. The right-hand *hu kou* is still attached to the tip of the left elbow. The eyes follow the palm movement.

FIGURE 30

30. Repulse Monkey

From the previous posture, draw the body and the left leg backward. Resume the left empty step with the left heel touching the ground and the toes pointing upward. The left palm is raised to ear level with the fingers pointing to the front. The right palm is pushed down to the right side of the hip.

FIGURE 31

31. Flying Oblique

From the previous posture, draw the left leg one step backward to form the right archery step. The right and left palm stay stationary, while the body weight is concentrated on the right leg. Then turn the waist and pivot the right foot on its heel to the southeast. Both palms are placed in front of the body, with the left palm facing upward and the right palm facing downward. The eyes are looking at the back of the right palm.

32. Flying Oblique

From the previous posture, draw the left leg one step to the northeast, with the left foot pointing to the southeast and parallel with the right foot. At the same time stretch the left arm backward.

FIGURE 32

The left palm is facing upward and the fingers are pointing to the northeast. The right arm stretches downward to the southwest with the palm pushing downward. The body weight is concentrated on the left leg; the eyes are looking at the back of the right palm.

The flying oblique is so named because the posture is shaped like a flying swallow. The idea is to attack the enemy with the left shoulder; this is called leaning, one of the eight basic techniques of tai chi. Use the strength of the waist and the opposing power of the arms to greatly increase the attacking force of the shoulder.

33. Needle at the Bottom of the Sea

From the left empty step, draw the left leg backward. The left foot is still empty, with the heel lifted and the toes lightly touching the ground.

FIGURE 33

The body weight is on the right leg. Then gradually bend the right knee and move the body vertically downward, slightly inclined to the east. At the same time drop the right arm with the right fingers pointing downward and slightly to the front. The left palm draws backward to the crook of the right elbow. The eyes look at the right palm.

This is one of the methods of using the plucking *(tsai)* force. If the opponent catches your right hand, divert it downward and make it fall into emptiness. Notice that the diverting energy is mainly created by the waist, not the right arm.

FIGURE 34

34. Fan Through the Back

From the previous posture, gradually raise the right arm to shoulder level with the left palm resting at the wrist of the right forearm. Then raise the left leg one step to the front, forming the left archery step. Turn the right palm to face front and gradually draw it to the right side of the forehead. The shape of the left palm is unchanged. At the same time pivot both legs on the heels to form the horse-riding posture. The eyes look at the back of the left palm.

Notice that the step follows the body turning. The energy is generated mainly by the turning of the waist. If the opponent attacks from the front, you can divert his attack with your right hand and counterattack with the left palm.

FIGURE 35

35. Parry and Punch

From the previous posture, drop the right palm in a circular movement to the left side of the body. Gradually form a fist. The left palm also gradually forms a fist and is dropped to the left side of the body. The fists are facing each other; the palms of the fists face downward, and the *hu kou* faces inward. At the same time pivot the left foot on its heel to the right; the body weight is concentrated on the left foot and the right foot becomes empty, ready to turn the body to the west. Make a punch with the back of the right fist.

There are five different punches in tai chi: parry and punch; step up and blocking punch; the planting punch; point to the crotch punch; and step forward, parry and punch. Each has defined characteristics and can be used in different situations.

36. Cloud Hands

From the posture single whip (Figure 6) open the right claw hand. The right palm is facing southwest. At the same time turn the waist

FIGURE 36

to the right and draw the left palm first downward and then upward to touch the wrist of the right hand. Following the body turning, pivot the left foot on its heel to the right. The feet are parallel, which point to the southwest. The weight is shifted to the bent right leg, which is solid. The straight left leg is empty. The eyes look at the back of the right palm.

37. Cloud Hands

From the previous posture, turn the body to the left to face southeast. At the same time pivot both feet on their heels to the left. The feet are parallel with the toes pointing southeast. The weight shifts to the left leg. Following the body turning, draw the left arm to the left with the palm facing inward. Finally, the left palm turns outward facing southeast, and the left arm is raised to the level of the left shoulder. The eyes look at the left palm when it turns to the left. The eyes look at the right palm when it turns to the right.

FIGURE 37

For martial arts purposes, the upper palm is used for diverting or plucking, while the lower hand is used for attacking. The hands work together. Cloud hands trains coordination. The eyes, hands, steps, and waist work together and follow each other. The turnings are made mainly by the waist.

38. High Pat the Horse

From the posture single whip (Figure 6), pivot the right foot on its heel to the east and draw the left foot about a half-foot backward. The toes touch the ground, with the heel up. At the

FIGURE 38

same time turn the body to the east, with the body weight resting on the right foot. The left foot is empty. Simultaneously draw the left arm backward to the left side of the body. The left forearm is bent up, forming a right angle with the upper left arm. The left palm is facing upward and the fingers are pointing to the front. The right palm is placed a fist distance above the left palm, which is facing east. The eyes look toward the southeast.

This method can be used for twisting. If the opponent punches at you from the front, receive the opponent's fist with your left hand and twist his elbow with your right palm.

FIGURE 39

39. The Right Parting Leg

From the previous posture, turn the palms in circular movements to the left side of the ear. The palms form fists and cross each other at the inner part of the wrists. The right fist is in front, facing inward, and the left fist is in back, facing outward. Both elbows form a 90-degree angle and are placed at the level of the shoulders. Move the left foot forward to form the left archery step. The eyes look southeast.

40. The Right Parting Leg

From the previous posture, open both fists and form the erect palms. Then stretch the left palm to the left,

FIGURE 40

with the fingers pointing to the north. The arm drops to shoulder level. At the same time stretch the right palm to the right with the fingers pointing to the southeast. The right arm is also placed at the level of the shoulder. Soon after opening the left and right fists, gradually raise the right leg to the southeast and kick with the instep. The weight is on the left leg. The eyes look to the southeast.

41. High Pat the Horse

This is the right-side high pat the horse. The method is the same as Figure 38, only the right arm is bent to the right side of the body. The left foot is empty, but the heel is lifted with the toes slightly touching the ground.

FIGURE 41

42. The Left Parting Leg

From the previous posture, turn the left palm upward and the right palm downward to be crossed at the side of the right ear. The inner part of the left wrist is facing inward and the right outward. The body is in right archery step and the palms form fists. The eyes look at the northeast.

FIGURE 42

FIGURE 43

43. The Left Parting Leg

From the previous posture, open both fists and form the erect palms. Then stretch the right palm to the south and the left palm to the northeast. The arms are dropped to the shoulder level, with the elbows slightly bent. At the same time gradually raise the left leg to the northeast and kick with the instep. The weight is on the right leg, the eyes look northeast.

FIGURE 44

44. Turn Body, Pedaling Foot

From the previous posture, turn the body to the west and kick with the left heel to the front. The body weight is on the right leg and eyes look to the west. This is called pedaling or stamping kick. According to the rule, if the kicking leg is placed in front of the body, you kick with the heel. If the kicking foot is placed behind your body, kick with your instep.

45. Step Up, Planting Punch

This method is used after the brush knee and twist step following the stamping kick. The left palm is used for diverting and the right fist for punching. The body weight sits on the right leg forming the left empty step.

FIGURE 45

46. Step Up, Planting Punch

Bend the left leg to form the left archery step. At the same time punch with the bottom part of the right fist downward. The method is so called because it resembles the movement of an Oriental planting a rice seedling into the earth. Transforming the empty step to the archery step increases the strength of the punch.

FIGURE 46

FIGURE 47

47. Retreat Step, Beat the Tiger

From the posture right parting leg (Figure 40), draw the right kicking leg backward to form the left archery step. The body turns to the southeast. The left palm is facing downward and the right palm facing upward. The eyes look southeast.

48. Retreat Step, Beat the Tiger

FIGURE 48

From the previous posture, draw the left leg backward to form the right archery step. At the same time stretch the left palm to the front. Both palms are facing downward, the eyes looking at the palms.

FIGURE 49

49. Retreat Step, Beat the Tiger

From the previous posture gradually draw the waist backward to the northeast. At the same time stretch the left hand to the top of the head with the palm facing outward. The right palm pushes downward. The body weight is concentrated on the left leg.

50. Retreat Step, Beat the Tiger

FIGURE 50

From the previous posture, turn the body to the east. At the same time both palms form fists. The left fist is at the top with the *hu kou* facing downward. The right fist is placed in front of the abdomen with the *hu kou* facing upward. The upper and the lower *hu kou* are facing each other. The right leg is bent and raised up with the toes pointing upward. The left knee is slightly bent, and the body weight sits on the left leg. The eyes look to the east. This is also called "beat the tiger" posture.

51. Parting the Wild Horse's Mane

From the right erect palm (Figure 4), drop the right arm to the top of the left knee. The palm is facing inward with the fingers are pointing to earth. Bend the left elbow and raise the left palm to the top of the right shoulder with the palm facing inward. The height of the left fingers should not exceed the top of the right shoulder. The eyes look northwest. The weight sits on the left leg.

FIGURE 51

52. Parting the Wild Horse's Mane

Turn the waist to the left, so the arms turn to the left side of the body above shoulder level. The palms cross each other, with the right palm facing inward and the left palm facing outward. The weight remains on the left leg. The eyes look southwest.

FIGURE 52

53. Parting the Wild Horse's Mane

Draw the right foot one foot-space to the right and front to form the large right archery step. The weight is shifted to the right foot. At the same time, the right palm stretches to the front, with the fingers pointing west. The left palm pushes downward. The eyes look at the back of the left palm.

FIGURE 53

FIGURE 54

54. Parting the Wild Horse's Mane

Turn the waist to the right. At the same time draw the right arm backward to the level of the left shoulder and the left palm rightward to the top of the right knee. The right palm faces downward. The left palm faces upward. The eyes look southwest.

55. Parting the Wild Horse's Mane

From the previous posture, draw the left foot one step to the front to form the large left archery step. At the same time stretch the left arm to the front with the fingers pointing to the west. The left arm is in line with the left leg. The height of the left hand is at the level of the left shoulder. At the same time the waist is also turned to the southwest. The right palm is pushed downward to the northwest in line with the right leg. The body weight is on the left leg. The eyes look at the back of the right palm.

FIGURE 55

Parting the wild horse's mane is the open-door method. There are three consecutive twist steps in this form, termed *xin bu,* which means "managing the steps." For instance, if the opponent attacks from the front with his right hand, divert it with your right hand using the plucking force. At the same time move your left leg one step forward to block the opponent's leg and attack with your left shoulder using the leaning force. Your rear arm pushes downward to create the *zu jing,* which means "supporting force." This increases the leaning force of your shoulder.

56. Jade Girl Works at the Shuttle

The method is also called "the four-corner shuttle." The four corners are southwest, southeast, northeast, and northwest.

This is the third of the four successive forms, which faces northeast. The posture is left archery step facing east. The upper body is turned to the northeast while the step is still to the east. The left arm is raised to the shoulder level, forming a semi-circle, with its palm facing northeast. The fingertips are in line with the nose. The right palm is pushed out under the middle portion of the left forearm, which faces northeast. The head and the eyesight are turned to the northeast. The body weight sits on the left leg.

FIGURE 56

57. Jade Girl Works at the Shuttle

This is the last of the four shuttle movements facing northwest. The posture is right archery step, facing west. The upper body is turned northwest with the palms pushing in the same direction. The head and eyes are turned northwest. The weight sits on the right leg.

FIGURE 57

58. Downward Posture

From the posture single whip (Figure 6), open the right claw hand and draw the right palm upward then downward to meet the wrist of the left hand. At the same time turn the waist to the east and the body weight is shifted to the left leg. Draw the waist backward and move the right foot about a half-step to the west. The body weight shifts to the right leg. The left leg is straight. The palms pull backward, and the eyes look at the left palm.

FIGURE 58

59. Golden Cockerel Standing on One Leg

From the previous posture, straighten the waist and raise the right leg to kick with the heel. The toes point upward. The weight sits on the left leg. The right palm is raised about one fist distance above the forehead, with the fingers point to the north. The left palm pushes downward with the fingers pointing south. The eyes look east.

FIGURE 59

60. Golden Cockerel Standing on One Leg

This is the front view of this form.

FIGURE 60

FIGURE 61

61. Palm to Meet the Face

The method is the continuation of the form high pat the horse (Figure 38). The left palm is pushed to the east at the level of the opponent's face. The right palm is placed under the left armpit facing downward. The body weight is on the left leg. The eyes look at the back of the left palm.

FIGURE 62

62. Turn Body, Single Lotus Kick

From the previous posture, pivot the left foot on its heel to the right and the body is turned to the west. Following the body turning, the left palm is also turned to the west with the fingers pointing north. The right palm is still under the left armpit. Raise the right leg to the left, then kick with the right instep from left to right in a circular movement. At the same time drop the left palm and slap the right instep.

FIGURE 63

63. Pointing to the Crotch Punch

The method is similar to the planting punch (Fig. 46) except that this punch uses the front part of the fist to attack the opponent's lower part of the abdomen.

64. Step Up to Form the Seven Star

From the downward posture (Figure 58), raise the right leg one step to the front, forming the right empty step, but the toes are touching the ground. At the same time raise both the right palm and

FIGURE 64

left palm to the front of the chest. With the left little finger placed on the root of the right thumb. The body weight is on the left leg. The eyes look east.

This is the closing-door method, which is expecting the enemy's attack from the front.

65. Retreat Step, Ride the Tiger

From the previous posture, draw the crossed palms downward and move the right empty leg backward to form the left archery step. Again, draw the body backward; the left archery step changes to left empty step. Then pivot the right foot on its heel to the south. At the same time flick the left leg and the hooked left foot upward to the right. Raise the arms to shoulder level. The left fingers form the hook hand, and the right hand forms the erect palm. The body weight is on the right leg. The eyes look east.

FIGURE 65

FIGURE 66

66. Turn Body, Hit the Face Palm)

From the previous posture, open the left claw hand and drop the left foot. Then turn the body rightward to face west. At the same time make a push to the west with the left palm to the opponent's face. The right palm is placed under the left armpit. The body weight is concentrated on the left leg and the eyes look at the left palm.

Notice that the turning is made on the right leg. The attacking force is increased by the centrifugal force created by the body turning.

FIGURE 67

67. Turn Body, Double Lotus Kick

This is the left empty step facing east. The weight is on the left leg. Both arms are stretched out to the south with the palms facing downward. When you raise the right leg to make a transverse kick, pat the instep of the right foot first with the left palm then the right palm, hence the name "double lotus kick."

If the enemy's attack comes from behind, turn the body and divert the attacking force with your palms. Then make a transverse kick to the enemy's abdomen with your right foot.

FIGURE 68

68. Curve Bow, Shoot Tiger

This is the right archery step facing east. The weight is concentrated on the right leg. The right fist is twisted and punches to the front at the level of your face. The right *hu kou* is facing downward. The left fist is dropped to the left side of the abdomen with its *hu kou* facing upward. The right and left *hu kou* are facing each other. Following the previous method, if the enemy continues to attack you can divert the attacking force with your left hand and punch the enemy's face with the right fist.

69. Closing Tai Chi

FIGURE 69

From the single whip posture, turn the waist to the south and draw the left leg to the front to form the parallel step. Then drop the arms and resume the posture of the beginning style. The feet are returned to where the exercise started.

CHAPTER 6

Push Hands: The Two-Person Tai Chi Practice

When I place my palm gently on a student's chest and say that my energy is already on his body, he replies, "Yes, you are pushing me." Then I add some of my sinking energy to the ground and the student is pushed outward. While I am doing this, the muscles of my arm are soft, my elbow bent, and my shoulder loose. I don't push him with my arm, I push him with my legs. What does it mean? Quite simply, I sink my energy to the ground mainly by my waist and the intentions of my mind.

The ground produces the reacting force that transmits through my legs, waist, arm, hand, and finally to the body of the student. It all happens at the same instant.

The more you apply the sinking energy, the stronger the reacting force. Thus, the acting force will be greater on the student. The mechanism is much like a moving car hitting a solid wall. On impact it will bounce off. I often explain this by using the phrase "borrowing strength from the earth." I have had many tai chi students since I came to the U.S. Some said they studied tai chi for ten or twenty years, but unfortunately, few understood the role of "rooting the legs." This means using the strength that comes from the ground.

Exercising on a machine is popular in the West. Rows of newly designed exercise machines are the totems of a health club. Many people also have an exercise machine of their own so they can work out in their homes. With a machine, people repeat the same mechanical work with their extremities. They stretch, pull, or step strenuously and continuously but rarely work the mind. Since they can read, watch television, or talk when they exercise, the muscles are the only things that get worked. Tai chi, on the other hand, is different because it uses the mind.

With the mind you direct the energy, and with the energy you direct the body. This creates a unity of mind, energy, and body. The exercise is diminished or totally ineffective if the mind is separated from the movements. Purely mechanical work is not natural. To separate the mind from the process is artificial, because it is not in accordance with the balance of yin and yang. If any single part of the body moves, all parts of the body move toward the same goal. If any single part of the body stops, all parts of the body stop at the same moment. Tai chi trains the whole being, mentally, spiritually, and physically.

Stillness and relaxation are the essence of tai chi. Stillness never means suspending the mind; in fact, during the state of stillness the mind is more sensitive, flexible, and capable of adapting to any external stimuli. This can be likened to a river that shines and reflects like mirror when it is calm, but distorts or obstructs the view if it is turbulent.

Relaxing the muscles facilitates transmission of the internal energy from joint to joint throughout the body according to the intention of the mind. It takes some time for a beginner to learn how to eliminate the rigidity of the muscles, especially the shoulder and waist muscles, and to help the body work as one entity.

In China, the human body has been acknowledged since ancient times as the microcosm of the universe. Like all things in the universe, all parts in the human body are continuously moving and changing according to the theory of yin and yang, which was described in the well-known ancient Chinese classic *I-Ching,* also called the *Book of Changes.*

The term "tai chi" was first introduced in the *I-Ching.* The ideas of integrity of the whole body, the continuous movements, and the differences of empty and solid (yin and yang) are based on the philosophy of this book. Tai chi exercise maintains longevity and eternal spring, which means that you can be vigorous and healthy as if you are always young. To maintain longevity is to follow the rule of nature, which is the harmony of yin and yang.

Through proficiency of the forms, you can gradually learn to manage the internal energy. This is called reaching a state of "strength perception." Through strength perception you may advance step by step to the ultimate goal—enlightenment.

Practiced skill, strength perception, and "enlightenment" constitute the three levels of learning tai chi.

The tai chi solo form is the foundation, while push hands, the method based on the solo forms, is the application. Thus, push hands is often acknowledged as the explanation of the forms.

Wu-style push hands is well-known for its softness, integrity, strict central equilibrium, and variety of the techniques.

The late grandmaster Wu Chian-chuan often advised his students learning push hands to first neutralize or divert the opponent's strength rather than use force to attack.

To neutralize or divert and then attack are opposite aspects of the yin and yang spectrum. However, if one is skilled in neutralization, one should also know how to attack. Contrary to conventional methods of combat, neutralizing always precedes attacking in tai chi. The practitioner should never strike first according to a fixed method that is irrelevant to the movement and intention of the opponent. It is better to follow and adhere to the attacking force—whether rapid or slow—and divert the opponent into a disadvantageous position while always maintaining your *zhong-din*.

THE BASIC PRINCIPLES OF PUSH HANDS

Overcome Hardness with Softness

A common saying in Chinese states, *"Rou overcomes gang."* The word *rou* means "soft and flexible." Gang is "hard and energetic." *Rou* is the negative force considered to be as the yin; *gang* is the positive force considered to be the yang.

In push hands, if the force is antagonistic, it is the *gang* force regardless of whether it is heavy or light. On the other hand, if your force is flexible or changeable, capable of increasing or decreasing according to your opponent's attacking force, it is *rou* strength.

When *gang* force confronts *gang* force, the one who possesses the greater physical strength will win. When confronted with the *gang* force, if you resist with your own strength by neglecting to go along with the incoming force or divert it into emptiness, the energy you use is called the dead force. The opposite is movable force. When dead force meets movable force it often results in emptiness by the movable force and eventually fails. This is the meaning of *rou* overcoming *gang*.

To apply the rule of *rou* overcoming *gang*, one should learn the method of diverting, and how to use the adhesion strength to seize an advantage, take a favorable position, and find time for an attack. Never use force against force or contend for a first strike; in such instances greater strength overcomes weaker strength and faster hands defeat slower hands. The principal role of push hands is to be flexible and neutralizing, always avoiding unnecessary and disadvantageous conflict with the opponent. It should be noted, however, that retreating or evading without attacking runs counter to the principles of push hands, which call for the interaction of *rou* and *gang*.

Meet the Offensive with Stillness

In martial arts, the aspects of empty and solid are contained in one's strength, not expressed in the external forms. It is not suitable to launch an attack if the opponent's strength is being reserved and his empty and solid points are not fully detected. It is also inappropriate to attack rashly if the opponent still can stretch out and draw back even if he is in a vulnerable position. In such instances, you may give the opponent an opening to counterattack. Let the opponent attack first; then, as if meekly submitting, lead him into the field of your attack. This is where diverting or plucking are best utilized.

Audible strength, a special term used in push hands, means to discover the intention, the orientation of the movements, and the points of void and solid in your opponent with your hands or body through the sensations of touching and feeling. It is as if you "hear" through the skin. Stillness is essential for managing the audible strength.

Without stillness, effective audible strength can hardly be attained.

Without audible strength your actions are made blindly and will not be enough to challenge your opponent.

A swift attack can be launched if, by using your audible strength, you find your opponent in a disadvantageous position and incapable of making a rapid change. Using a tai chi term called *jee,* which means "opportunity," it will be easy for you to hit at the right point, because of your favorable time and position. In case you don't hit the target, you're out of range of a counterattack because of his disadvantageous position.

Overcome the Opponent with Lesser Strength but Better Skill

Tai chi's martial arts aspect manifests itself externally in the forms, referred to as *zhe,* which means "measure." What is present internally is the *jin* or the strength. It is this interaction of the *zhe* and *jin* that composes the unique martial arts aspects of tai chi. The skill of using lesser strength to subdue a stronger opponent is well-known within tai chi circles. Apply your *zhe* to the opponent and increase or decrease your internal *jin* to upset his center of gravity. Or you may divert first and adhere and follow his movements until he reaches an adverse or vulnerable position. You may then take advantage of his movements and knock him down easily even with a single touch of the hand.

Retreat to Advance

The Classics say, "To join the hardness with softness is to go along with. To treat the adverse when you are in the advantageous position is sticking to it." Going along with and sticking are the two main strategies in push hands. To go along with is to neutralize the opponent. To stick is to control the opponent. It is the interaction of the going along with and sticking to that produces the ever-changing patterns of push hands. The circular movements of tai chi can be found in the symbol of tai chi. The movements are constantly evolving and comprise innumerable changes of moving and adhering within the circle. Learning to adapt to changing conditions is important with push hands.

When confronted by an opponent you should know the direction and quality of his strength through your "audible" ability. The main strategy is to follow. The energy you use will be either energetic or flexible, or *gang* and *rou*. If both sides use *gang* force, there will be no way to follow, which means you are unable to go along with. You are unable to divert without going along with; unable to adhere without diverting; and unable to detect the intention of the opponent through your audible strength. If a rash attack is made in such an instance, the one with greater strength will win.

Going along with diverts the opponent's energy, safeguards you from the opponent's attack, and transforms your condition of passivity into activity. Adhesion continues to control the opponent with the advantage you reached through diverting. This is the meaning of retreating to advance.

The Classics also say, "If the opponent doesn't move , I don't move. If the opponent starts to move, I move ahead of him." But if neither side is ready to move, and if the condition is a stalemate, you may start the attack by using the strategy of "retreat to advance." If there is no response from the opponent to your feint you may give a real strike. If the opponent resists with force you may change your hand into emptiness and take advantage of his exposed force to launch a second attack.

The Circular Movements

Tai chi features the characteristic of circular movements. Circular movements are easy to transform from *rou* into *gang* or vice versa. Alternating changes of hardness and flexibility, or "going along with" and "sticking to" are based on the circular movements. Circular movements can be faster and can more easily reach the opponent than a straight back-and- forth attack because there is no pause or breaking of strength during the action. In tai chi language this is called "starting late but reaching first." Generally, the first half of the circle is for diverting and the last half is for attacking.

The higher the level of skill of a tai chi master, the smaller the circle he will make. Sometimes there is only the sense of a circular movement, with no curved lines manifested externally; this is because the master mainly uses his internal energy.

The Strength of Center of Gravity

The weight of any body part is produced by the gravity of the Earth. During exercise the center of gravity of all parts of the body falls vertically to the ground despite the changing of posture. They form a complex vector within the body, and the forces meet each other at a point called the center of gravity. In other words, the center of gravity is the point of acting force where all the gravity forces in all parts of the body meet. With the legs as support, a person can stand, but the vertical line from the center of gravity must be dropped within the supporting space of the legs. If it exceeds the area of the supporting space, one is bound to fall. There are two ways to ensure the stability of the center of gravity: to lower the center of gravity, and to enlarge the area of the supporting space.

Bending the knees or sinking the energy to the lower part of the abdomen can also accomplish lowering the center of gravity. Gymnasts and others such as Beijing opera actors who perform somersaults may have an advantage if they are shorter, because of their lower center of gravity. The supporting space of the legs cannot be enlarged at will. If the distance of the legs is extended vertically, there will be a decrease in the area transversely. If the distance between the legs is enlarged transversely, there will be a decrease in the area vertically. The narrow side is called the weak point in push hands, which easily loses the center of gravity if attacked. The meaning of the changing of empty and solid foot, either in the solo form or during push hands, is to stabilize the center of gravity by adapting the body to the supporting space of the legs. When performing a high-wire walking act, an acrobat often holds a long pole to lower his center of gravity. A more-skilled acrobat may walk on the high wire without a pole; much depends on the way he changes his footing to maintain his center of gravity. The effects are similar to the change of empty and solid steps in tai chi.

The Role of "Coupling"

"Couple" is a mechanical term denoting two parallel and equal forces acting in opposite directions, but not in a straight line. Using couple force is frequently encountered in daily life. For instance, when you turn the key to open the door you hold the key with two fingers; the applied forces at the two points are the same but go in opposite directions, thus the key is turned smoothly without using much force. Other examples include turning off a faucet or guiding the steering wheel. There are many movements in tai chi that use the couple force, such as "high pat the horse" and "right and left open body." During push hands, when you stroke the shoulders of the opponent with your hands at the same time, your right palm strokes his left shoulder downward and the left palm pushes his right shoulder upward. The hands interact in a circular movement that forms the couple force. Because it is difficult to adapt the body to two different forces at the same instant, it will be hard for the opponent to change this disadvantageous position.

Impulse and Momentum

The intensity of the impulse is equal to the product of the acting force and acting time. Thus, the longer the acting time, the stronger the impulse force will be. The techniques of adhesion and following in push hands are said to increase the attacking force because of the longer acting time. This is one reason why you can defeat an opponent when you have lesser strength but superior skill. That's also why a flexible-handled hammer will crush a stone easier than a straight and hard-handled variety.

The word "momentum" denotes the force gained by movement. As a rock rolls down a mountainside, the movement becomes faster and faster because of gathered momentum. In push hands the main strategy is to take advantage of the opponent and push in the same direction of his movement. The effect is to increase and accelerate his momentum. The opponent will fall by himself because of his increased momentum.

THE THIRTEEN BASIC MOVEMENTS

Warding (the peng force)

This is considered to be concealed strength because the method is based on your feeling. It is barely expressed in the external movements. It ranks first in the thirteen basic movements, indicating its importance. Beginners usually require years of practice to accomplish the basic skill of the *peng* force. *Peng* force appears empty but is solid in reality and vice versa. With *peng* force, you can feel the strength and intentions of your opponent while your own strength and intentions are kept hidden. During push hands, any part of the body, including the hands and arms, that comes into contact with the opponent should make use of *peng* force. *Peng* strength has also been called supporting force. It is like water in the river, which carries a tiny leaf but also floats a thousand-ton boat. *Peng* force is created mainly through tai chi skill. The strength needed for your *peng* force depends on the opponent. If the oncoming force is heavy, your *peng* strength should also be raised; if the oncoming force is light, it should be decreased. Your *peng* strength, however, should never exceed the opponent's force.

Rather, it is lighter than the oncoming force. *Peng* force is not resisting, nor escaping. The purpose is to prevent the opponent from reaching your body. Even if you attack, your *peng* force will make it difficult for your opponent to escape or strike back.

Diverting (the *lu* force)

This is the overt force. When the direction and force of the opponent's attack have been detected by your warding force, divert it to the side of your body and lure him into continuing despite his reaching an adverse position. When his oncoming force reaches its end, it naturally becomes broken force, which tells you the time to make a counterattack.

Pressing (the *ji* force)

It is the overt force, also called the "pressing the elbow" technique, which is one of the expert techniques in Wu-style push hands. If the opponent diverts your right arm, bend your right elbow and follow the opponent's diverting. At the same time draw your left palm to the crook of the right elbow and press with the bottom side of your left palm. Use the back palm to press at the elbow of the front arm. The same method can be used if the opponent is diverting the left arm.

Pushing (the *an* force)

This is the overt force. If the opponent attacks with pressing, you push his arm or chest downward to uproot him and weaken his pressing force. If the opponent retreats, you can continue your pushing to the front and upward, preventing him from taking even a single breath to change. The pushing is made in a wave-like or undulating form.

Plucking (the *tsai* force)

This is the semi-overt and semi-concealed force. It is like plucking fruit from a tree. Handle the fruit gently at first, then pluck with a sudden draw or tug. If your arm is at the top of the opponent, you can pluck him in the oblique direction. This is called the upper plucking and is the overt strength. If your hand is below the opponent, you can divert his attack with the supporting force and attack with other strength. This is the lower plucking and is the concealed force.

Twisting (the *li* force)

This is overt force. Take advantage of the opponent's oncoming force and twist his forearm, elbow, and hand with your hands. The opponent's elbow and shoulder will be blocked, become rigid, and will easily be thrown out by your twisting.

Elbowing (the *zhou* force)

This is the overt force. Using the outer surface of your bent forearm to stick to the opponent's forearm and attack his weak point is called attacking with the elbow. When following the oncoming force, stick the outer surface of your upper arm to the outer surface of the opponent's elbow and press it to the side of your body. This is called diverting with the elbow.

Using the elbow is another of the expert techniques in Wu-style push hands. The methods are profound, subtle, and varied. Elbowing can also be used in combination with other manipulations such as pressing, pushing, plucking, or twisting.

Leaning (the *kao* force)

This is overt strength. When you are confronted with a swift attack and it is too late to change your hands, you may use the opponent's force to counterattack with your back or shoulder. The leaning force is swift and heavy, which may vigorously shake the opponent.

Jin (stepping forward)

This is the overt strength. The method is to step forward to chase the retreating opponent. You also use the adhesion strength to prevent the opponent from escaping.

Tui (stepping backward)

This is the overt force. If the opponent is attacking fiercely, you step back to neutralize the offensive. It is not running away. As a Classic says, "To meet the hardness with softness is to go along with."

Ku (looking to the left)

This is the overt force. If the opponent attacks from the right, you turn 90 degrees to the left and look at him to see the response.

Pan (looking to the right)

This is the overt force. If the opponent attacks from the left, you turn 90 degrees to the right and look at him to see his next attempt.

Din (the abbreviation of *zhong-din*)

This is the concealed force. *Zhong-din* is the most basic skill of tai chi. It is the governing principle of the thirteen kinetic movements. The other twelve movements are the subordinate. Without *zhong-din* the alternative variations of empty and solid do not exist. Whenever there is empty and solid there is the *zhong-din*. None of the twelve basic movements can ever be dissociated from *zhong-din*. Strictly speaking, there is no fixed method for any movement, but all the forms or movements must be based on *zhong-din*.

OPENING THE FOUR DOORS

Self-Training Method of Warding, Diverting, Pressing, and Pushing

The method of learning the four orthodox methods of push hands—warding, diverting, pressing, and pushing—has been traditionally called opening the four doors. The self-training method is the preparation for the two-man push hands. For the purpose of preciseness and regularity it is preferable for students to start from the self-training method. This is also the way to practice the basic skills of push hands when a partner is not available.

The following shows Master Ma Yueh-liang demonstrating the self-training method of the four orthodox methods of push hands.

FIGURE 1

FIGURE 1 Stand upright and maintain *hui-ling-din-jin*. The eyes look a bit downward, forming about a 25-degree angle to the ground. The shoulders are loose and one stands with the parallel step. From the parallel step stretch the left leg to the front with the heel touching the ground and the toes pointing forming the left empty step.

The right knee is a little bent, and the body weight sits on the right leg to form the left empty stance. Simultaneously raise both palms upward and forward. Both hands form the erect palm. The left palm is placed at the top of the right palm; the height of the fingers does not exceed the shoulders. The right palm is placed at the level of the curve of the left elbow, which is facing left.

FIGURE 2

FIGURE 2 From the left empty step, push the palms downward, with the forearms forming right angles with the upper body. The right palm faces downward and the left palm upward.

FIGURE 3

FIGURE 3 From the above left empty step, bend the left leg to the front to form the left archery step. At the same time draw both arms to the front to form a circle. The left palm is in front of the right arm, facing inward. The bottom edge of the right palm is placed at the curve of the left elbow, forming the press elbow posture. The height of the arms is at the level of the shoulders.

FIGURE 4

FIGURE 4 From the above posture, drop the left arm and stretch the left palm forward with the fingers pointing to the front. The right palm is still placed at the curve of the left elbow. The left archery step remains unchanged.

From the above posture draw the body backward to resume the posture of Figure 2. Then the exercise can be done continuously and repeatedly.

In Memory of Grandmaster Ma Yueh-liang

On the weekend of March 14, 1998, I received bad news by e-mail from my daughter in Shanghai that 98-year-old Master Ma Yueh-liang had died. He was diagnosed with colon cancer, and he died on March 13 in the hospital from renal failure after surgery.

Master Ma was my primary tai chi teacher in the 1930s, when I was teenager. My high school classmates and I were interested in tai chi chuan, which had spread to Shanghai from Beijing only a few years earlier. I wrote a letter to the Chian Chuan Association, and Master Ma was sent to teach us, a group of fewer than ten students. We practiced three times every week early in the morning in Wayside Park, which is now called the Labour Park, near our school.

Not long after the start of the Sino-Japanese war, Shanghai was occupied by the Japanese. Ma left Shanghai and walked through several interior provinces to reach Chungking, the wartime capital of the Chinese government.

During this long trip, he went through more than twenty pairs of cloth shoes. Sometimes he had to demonstrate martial arts in the city streets to earn money. This is one of the many interesting stories he told me later.

I was a medical student during the eight-year war. I lost contact with him and didn't know where he was. After the liberation, when the communists ruled China, I was working in a government hospital in the city center of Shanghai, located just behind the famous People's Park.

One day I passed the park and saw Master Ma teaching tai chi. His sturdy body structure, always-calm face, and his pure Beijing dialect were unmistakable. He had changed very little.

We were so happy to see each other after more than ten years of being apart. After that, I was a regular student. I also invited him to teach the doctors and nurses in our hospital.

Master Ma was not a medical doctor; he never treated patients, except those learners who had pain in their backs or extremities. His special field was laboratory work. He worked in the laboratory of the Shanghai Red Cross Hospital when he first came to Shanghai in the late 1920s.

The Chian Chuan Tai Chi Chuan Association was officially reestablished in 1980. Masters Wu Ying-hua and Ma Yueh-liang were the director and deputy director, respectively. I became one of the trustees and worked as the editor of its newsletter.

Since then, I had studied and worked with him even more closely. We were the co-authors of the book *Wu-Style Push Hands,* which was published in both Chinese and English in Hong Kong. I also translated his book *Wu-Style Tai ChiChuan: Forms, Concepts, and Application of the Original Wu-Style* into English.

This book is well known in the tai chi community in the United States, Germany, Australia, and areas in Southeast Asia.

Dr. Zee, Master Wu Yin-hua (Ma's wife), Master Ma, 1981. On the boat at the *Chang Fen Park* in Shanghai.

Later, I felt it a great honor to be accepted by Master Ma as one of his indoor students. An indoor student is usually selected after the teacher's long-time observation and consideration of the student's personal behavior and morals, as well as his attitude towards learning.

Master Ma probably had tens of thousand of students who took his classes, but there are only two or three dozen indoor students. Ever since the late 1980s, when Ma declared that his door was closed, no more indoor students were accepted.

An indoor student is a disciple who learned the authentic art from the teacher, called *sifu* in Chinese. He or she is the designated successor of the skills and characteristics of the *sifu*. "Indoor" means to enter the core of any school of art or craftsmanship, such as painting, Beijing opera, or martial art.

An indoor student shares the same lineage of the teacher. For instance, Chuan Yu was the founder of the Wu style. His son Wu Chian-chuan was the second generation, Ma Yueh-liang was the third generation, and Ma's indoor students are the fourth generation.

In either the Yang style or the Wu style, when a master selects an indoor student, a solemn ceremony takes place. A tablet, written with the name of Chang San-feng, the legendary founder of tai chi, is placed on the table in the center of the room. A pair of large red candles burns brightly in front of the tablet.

The new disciple has to kowtow or bow on the knees first to the tablet and then to the *sifu*. The *sifu* then instructs the student in disciplines such as how to pay respect to the teacher and how to help other indoor students whenever they have difficulties, because now they are joined in a fraternity forever.

More important are the secret passwords and the special signs or manners that the student should use when he is in a public place. The passwords are the same to all the indoor students and are strictly confidential; they should not be revealed to outdoor people, not even to one's own spouse or children.

The indoor students can recognize each other through the passwords, and help each other whenever they have difficulties, especially when one is far away from home.

Master Ma told me the story that once when he had his lunch in a restaurant in Guilin during his long trip to Chungking, he found out that his lunch had been paid for by someone just before he finished his meal. He talked to that man and immediately found out that they were brothers and had come from the same generation of the Wu school of tai chi chuan.

Master Ma was born into a martial arts family. His uncle was a general in charge of defending the entire city of Beijing. The wall of the city had nine gates, so he was called "the nine-gates general." His home had a very large yard, which served as a training ground for riding horses and shooting arrows.

When he was very young, Master Ma learned the hard martial art, tong bei ch'uang. At the age of twenty he changed to tai chi chuan taught by Master Wu Chian-chuan. In 1930, he married Master Wu Chian-chuan's daughter, Wu Yin-hua.

Master Ma's birthday is June 6 on the Chinese lunar calendar, which is about one month ahead on the solar calendar. A couple of years ago on July 6 his students organized a big party at the Political Consultative Hall of the Xu Hui district of Shanghai.

About two hundred people attended the party and sang "Happy Birthday," both in English and Chinese. He was in high spirits. He stood up many times to toast everyone and to thank them. We all looked forward to celebrating his 100th birthday with him, which was only two years away.

Now he has unexpectedly passed away. I lost my life-long teacher, and the tai chi world has lost a living treasure. I am concerned that his high-level skill will follow him into the ground, be buried, and will not be seen again.

When I saw the bad news from the e-mail, hot tears filled my eyes. I sat staring at the computer screen for a long time, grieving about the huge loss involved in his passing.

In 1997, I led an eighteen-member group on a visit to China. Sunday, October 5, was the day the Chian Chuan Association had its regular monthly demonstration meeting in the park. This time, my American students demonstrated two parts of the Wu-style slow form. Ma took the microphone and made a longer-than-usual explanation while we were performing.

Finally, Ma rose from the chair and performed push hands with six people, one after another without resting. He looked as if he were an old pine tree on the top of Yellow Mountain, standing gracefully and energetically under the blowing wind.

My American friends were wide-eyed with wonder watching Ma's push hands. They realized that they were seeing, for the first time, what true push hands looks like. They flew back via Beijing to Los Angeles about a week later, and I stayed a few extra weeks with my family in Shanghai.

The first Sunday of November was again the Association's open demonstration meeting. This time it was held in the square in front of the newly built National Events Stadium.

That day the weather was excellent, the sun shined brightly, and Ma arrived and pushed hands with seven people. I brought my 35mm camera, as well as my videorecorder and took as many valuable pictures of Ma's performance as I could.

A week after the meeting, I went to Ma's home. He was lying on his bed. He told me he suffered frequent bleeding from his hemorrhoid. I found out that it was unlike a simple hemorrhoid problem and suggested that he go to the hospital for a check-up. His eldest daughter and the youngest son took him by taxi to the hospital immediately. That was the last time I ever saw him. I had to fly back to America because of the date on my plane ticket. My biggest regret was that I didn't visit him often during my stay in Shanghai. I have written this article to honor him, and to express my deep sorrow for the loss of my teacher.

One of the characteristics of Ma's push hands is lightness.

When I pushed hands with him, I felt as if I were touching a piece of floating wood on the surface of water, unable to find any solid area on his body. But at the same time, his energy already reached the bottom of my feet. I felt uncomfortable in my legs and had to move or change my step.

Most amazing are the instances when Ma would spin people horizontally and they would fall onto their bottoms. One man was spiraled down and fell onto the ground.

As he stood, he began rubbing the area of pain. Clearly his buttocks were hurt. Ma could also tumble an opponent vertically, causing him to roll back two or three times. Those skills are definitely difficult to learn.

To my understanding, the cause of the spiraling and rolling was that Ma's energy was consistent with the force and direction of the opponent's energy.

When the opponent began turning, Ma added to that inertia or momentum by using his intention of wanting to help the opponent on his way in that turning motion. Actually, the opponent fell through his own force.

One tai chi participant told me, after tumbling backwards, "It's strange; I could never do a back roll on my own, but Ma sent me into one and I did not hurt myself."

The three series of pictures included here show Ma's last push hands performance. A few days after this he went into the hospital.

The still camera doesn't capture the subtleties of his movements. Fortunately, I have videotape showing the action, which will be my most valuable memento of Master Ma.

FIGURE A1

FIGURE A2

FIGURE A3

FIGURE A4

THE FIRST SERIES OF PHOTOS:

A1: At the first touch of Ma's hand, his energy is already at the opponent's feet. Notice that the opponent's feet are shaking, and look at how stable Ma is on his feet. Also, notice that there are people standing around them to protect the opponent from injury in case he is thrown or falls.

A2: Ma's diverting *(lu)* further causes the opponent to be off-balance. Ma uses very little energy, and his left hand does not even touch the opponent. This because Ma is sensing and using his energy to move the opponent in the direction the opponent tends to go.

A3: The opponent is attempting to divert Ma's right arm. Ma uses pressing *(ji)* strength. The Wu-style pressing uses the back palm to press at the curve of the front arm inside the elbow. In the picture, Ma has not used his left hand yet.

A4: Ma uses typical *ji* method. The opponent is thrown.

FIGURE B1

FIGURE B2

FIGURE B3

FIGURE B4

THE SECOND SERIES OF PHOTOS:

B1: After the first contact, the opponent loses his balance, and his body shifts to Ma's left side. Ma uses mental energy or will power with his right finger pointing to his left side to enhance the opponent's shifting.

B2: When the opponent starts to fall forward, he suddenly pulls himself backward. Ma uses the opponent's own force and pushes *(an)* at the opponent's turning direction. The opponent flies backward.

B3: Ma's right hand and his senses are still concentrating on the center of the opponent. The opponent continues to fly backward, even though Ma didn't touch his body.

B4: The opponent begins to jump back, and hops on one leg in an effort not to fall. This jumping method is often used by practitioners when they are off-balance in push hands.

FIGURE C1

FIGURE C2

FIGURE C3

FIGURE C4

THE THIRD SET OF PHOTOS:

C1: The opponent's upper body is already shifting to Ma's right side by Ma's diverting (*lu*), but he tries hard to stand firm in his horse-riding stance.

C2: Ma suddenly turns his waist to his left, and the opponent is uprooted. See how the opponent's toes are pointed and blurred, indicating the movement upward from the ground. Ma has broken the opponent's connection with the ground.

C3: While the opponent is flying backward from a push *(an)*, Ma's right index finger points to the opponent, and he uses his mental energy to accelerate the opponent's backward movement.

C4: At last the opponent tumbles to the ground, rolling backward twice.

Glossary

An Literally means "push." It is one of the four basic techniques in push hands. The others are *peng, lu,* and *tsee. An* or the push can be made with one or both hands.

Banner The waist is described in the tai chi classics as the banner, referring to the big flag that was held by the commander to direct the soldiers on the battlefield in ancient times. The soldiers must move and fight according to the direction pointed out by the banner.

Centered Tail Bone The tail bone is the bottom end of the spine. If the tail bone is centered the spine will be straight. If the spinal is twisted the tail bone will not be centered.

Chen Jin The word *chen* means "sink," and *jin* is "strength." *Cheng jin* literally means to sink the energy to the ground. Your body weight, including the internal organs is always pulled downward by the gravity of the Earth. This is nature's way. While your body weight sinks to the ground, the Earth also creates the rebound force so that you can stand upright. Your sinking strength can be increased through the practice of tai chi, by relaxing the muscles, using abdominal breathing, and focusing the intention of the mind. The greater the sinking strength, the stronger the reacting force. The common saying in tai chi "borrow strength from the earth" denotes the effect of *chen jin,* or the sinking force.

Ding Jin The pulling or supporting strength created by the top of the head. The goal is to straighten the spine and enable the pulling strength of the head and the sinking strength of the body to complement each other and work together as one entity. The tai chi classics describe the top of the head as if hanging by a string from heaven. Hence the term *din tou yuan,* which means "the top of the head is hanging up." This method is very important in maintaining the body's central equilibrium, both in practicing the forms and push hands.

Duan Jin Literally means "broken strength." It is well known that the energy and the movements should be made continuously without interruption, as described in the Classics like pulling silk from a cocoon. *Duan jin* is one of the common errors in practice that should always be avoided. Even the movement reaches its end, the sense of continuity remains.

Double-Weighting The movements of the arms or legs without empty and solid, or yin and yang, is called "double-weighting." This is another common error in practice that should be avoided.

Erect Palm Stretch the right palm about one foot distance in front of the nose with the palm facing left, and the fingers pointing slantingly upward. If the left palm is used, it faces right. The erect palm is often used to receive the strength of the opponent for the purposed of diverting or neutralizing.

Fa Jing Literally means "launching energy" for an attack. It is wrong to consider that the movements of tai chi are always soft and never use force. Lightness and using force are the yin and yang. Yin and yang always complement each other. Without one the other will not exist. Actually, launching strength with tai chi can be extremely powerful because the whole body works together for the same purpose, and the force is concentrated in one direction.

Hang-Shung-Ba-Bei Literally means "raise the back and empty the chest." Because the energy is sinking to the *dan tian* (lower part of the abdomen), the chest can't be puffed out as Westerners usually do. The back is pulled up by the head, which produces the opposing force while sinking energy to the *dan tian.*

Hui-lin-Din-Jin Literally means "erect head and empty neck." The top of the head is held as if it were hanging from heaven, while the strength of the body sinks downward to the earth. This produces the opposing force of the body, which is critical in maintaining the body's central equilibrium.

Hu Kao Literally means "the mouth of the tiger." This is the area where the root of the thumb and the index finger join at the edge of the palm. The two fingers form an angle and always open and close simultaneously as necessary.

Jee Literally means "pressing." This is one of the distinguishing features of the Wu-style push hands, often called "pressing the elbow." During push hands if the opponent diverts your right arm, you bend your right arm, and let it go along smoothly with the opponent's diverting force. But at the same time you apply the edge of your left palm to the curve of your right elbow, not necessarily using force. By doing so you have already gained the advantage. If the opponent continues his diverting, he is pulling his own body backward, you can easily push him out by merely adding some pressing strength with your left palm. The same method can be applied if the opponent diverts your left arm.

Jin The word literally means "strength or force." Because of the unique way using force in tai chi, people like to use the word *jin,* instead of force, to distinguish it from the raw force that is created by the mechanical movements that are made by the extremities alone.

Kao Literally means "leaning." This is one of eight movements of tai chi, namely, *peng* (warding), *lu* (diverting), *jee* (pressing), *an* (pushing), *tsai* (plucking), *li* (twisting), *zhou* (elbowing), and *kao* (leaning). The effect of leaning is to attack with your shoulder or the back.

Li Literally means "twisting." There are variations in the methods. The commonly used technique is to hold the arm of the opponent at two points with your hands and twist it to block the joint of his elbow or shoulder.

Listening Strength In Chinese this is popularly called *tin jin.* The word *tin* means "to listen or hear," and *jin* is the "strength." *Tin jin* is one of the basic skills in push hands. The purpose is to find out the intention and quality of the opponent's attacking force, which includes its intensity, direction, and the solid and empty points through your own touching and feeling. It is much like to hear something from the opponent, hence the term *listening strength.*

Lu Literally means "diverting." This is the commonly used term in push hands. The purpose is to divert the opponent's force into emptiness, or to neutralize his attacking force. The main point is that you are using the opponent's attacking force and avoid exposing your own strength. It takes some time for beginners to grasp the essence of diverting.

Ming Men Literally means "life gate." It is the point located at the back of the waist outside spine. While you are making a push to the front, the area of *ming men* stick out to create the opposing force.

Opposing Force The classics say "if there is something in the front, there must be something in the back; if there is something on the left, there must be something on the right; and if there is something on the top, there must be something on the bottom. This forms the opposing force, which means there are two forces that go in opposite directions and balance each other. The opposing force has the effects of elongation of the muscles and joints and promoting the body's central equilibrium. The circular movements made by the arms also create a couple. The couple is a special term used in physics to refer to a pair of forces of equal magnitude acting in parallel and opposite directions and capable of causing rotation. The opposing forces used in tai chi often form a couple and the methods are frequently encountered in daily life, such as turning a key with two fingers to open the door, moving a steering wheel or turning a faucet on and off.

Peng The *peng* force ranks first of the eight kinetic movements, and this shows its importance. Some authors also claim that tai chi is actually the martial arts of the *peng* force. The *peng* strength is usually called the "warding force" in English. The word *peng* did not exist in original Chinese. It is a special term with complex meanings that can only be applied in tai chi. In push hands any part of the body that connects with the opponent should apply the *peng* strength. It may be compared with the buoyancy of water in a river. On it drifts a tiny leaf, but it also can carry a ten-thousand-ton boat. The *peng* strength is relatively difficult for the beginners to learn. It is said that only when the student understands the *peng* force may he be considered to have acquired the rudiments of tai chi.

Qi-Chen-Dan-Tian The word *qi* means "energy," and *chen* is "sinking." *Dan tian* is the acupuncture point located about two inches under the umbilicus, believed to be the area where the body's center of gravity is located. Sinking the energy to the *dan tian* enhances the sinking force and is also essential for abdominal breathing.

Sheng Fa The word *sheng* means "body" and *fa* is the method. During push hands, not only the hands or the arms but any part of the trunk which connects to the opponent can be used for diverting or attacking, hence the term *sheng fa*.

Tsai The word *tsai* means "to pull with a sudden draw or tug." It is like plucking fruit from a tree: the hand holds the fruit gently at first, then pulls with a sudden tug. The movement is made quickly, like plucking feathers from a dead hen or duck.

Zhong-Din The word *zhong* literally means "centered," and "din" stability. *Zhong-din* is the most essential and basic skill of tai chi. It is more than the common idea of balance or central equilibrium, because it is the combination of the mind's intention, the internal energy, the empty and solid points, the eight directions and five steps, all working together as one entity. It cannot be reached solely through external mechanical work, it is organic. It should always be maintained despite the continuous changes of the body positions. It is true that there is no fixed method for push hands, but either push hands or practice the forms, should always be based on *zhong-din*.

Zhou The word *zhou* literally means "elbow." The Wu-style tai chi is well known for the variations of using the elbows, such as the methods of erect elbow, the central flat elbow, divert with elbow, and attack with elbow.